PATAGONIA

Windswept Land of the South

PATAGONIA

Windswept Land of the South

ROGER· PERRY

ILLUSTRATED WITH PHOTOGRAPHS AND A MAP

BBSL
· 9/91
· VPL book sale
- see also Bruce Chatwin's
"In Patagonia"

Dodd, Mead & Company · NEW YORK

PHOTOGRAPH CREDITS
Jeffery Boswall, page 15, 49, 95, 116; Courtesy of Juan Preloran, page 29 (top), 30; Peter Radcliffe, page 79, 84. All other photographs are by Roger Perry.

Map by Donald Pitcher.

Frontispiece: *The Strait of Magellan at Punta Arenas. Its importance as an international shipping route declined with the opening of the Panama Canal.*

Acknowledgments

I wish to thank Mr. Jeffery Boswall, Mr. Juan Preloran and Mr. Peter Radcliffe for their assistance with photographs used in this book. I am further grateful to Mr. and Mrs. William Pakenham Bridges for the kindest of hospitality in Tierra del Fuego; to Captain Tulio Rojas and members of the III Naval Zone of the Chilean Navy for many courtesies during my travels by sea; and to Miss Rosanne Lauer, Mr. Peter Hobbs, Dr. David Moore, and Mr. Eric Shipton for their many helpful comments and improvements to the text. To all these I extend my most appreciative thanks.

Contents

PATAGONIA
Windswept Land of the South

N

San Martín
de los Andes

Lake Nahuel Huapi

San Carlos de Bariloche
Llao-Llao
Mt. Tronadore
El Bolsón

Puerto Montt

Strait of Chacao

Ancud
Castro
Huequi Volcano

Island of Chiloé

△ *Minchinmávida Volcano*

Esquel

Yelcho L.

Negro R.

Viedma

Valdés Peninsula

Puerto Madryn

Gaiman Trelew

Chubut R.

FLORENTINO
AMEGHINO
DAM

Punta Tombo

Bustamante Bay

Chonos Archipelago

Puerto Aisén

Comodoro Rivadavia

Taitao Peninsula

Isthmus of Ofqui

Gulf of Peñas

Wager I.

Baker R.

Chico R.

Deseado R.

Puerto Deseado

**Pacific
Ocean**

Cerro
Torre
Mt. Fitz Roy

Lake
O'Higgins

Puerto
Edén

Wellington I.

Madre de Dios

Diego de Almagro

Lake
Viedma
Lake
Argentino

Santa Cruz R.

San Julián

Atlantic Ocean

Calafate

△ *Paine Mts.*
Mylodon Cave

Last Hope Inlet

Río Turbio
Puerto Natales

Río Gallegos

ARGENTINA
CHILE

Cape Virgins

Strait of Magellan

Mt.
Burney

Smyth Channel

*Muñoz Gamero
Peninsula*

The Evangelists

*Riesco
Island*

Punta Arenas
Porvenir

San Sebastián Bay

Desolation Island

Brunswick Peninsula

Port Famine (Fort Bulnes)

Río Grande

*Cape
Froward*

Useless Bay

Santa Inés Island

Dawson

Isla Grande

Clarence I.

Mt. Darwin

Lake Fagnano

Mitre Peninsula

Ushuaia
Wulaia

Staten Island

Tierra del

Darwin Range

*Hoste
Island*

Beagle Channel

Novarino Island

Fuego

Cape Horn

⬭ **PATAGONIA**

0   50   100   150
MILES

⬚ Glaciers, Ice Fields

Don Pitcher

1

Journey to the
Strait of Magellan

Patagonia is the region at the far south of the American continent. It is shared between Argentina and Chile and runs at its tip into the bleak archipelago known as Tierra del Fuego. This whole region was for me, for many years, a place of intriguing mysteries. It seemed to offer such contrasts in terrain and climate that it was difficult to form any precise idea of what to expect there. On one hand, I had been brought up with a picture of the great plains of southern Argentina, with their strange animals and mounted herdsmen riding over a sea of waving grasses. This I had to reconcile with what I knew of the country lying to the west, along the mountains bordering the Pacific. There, the picture was even more uncertain. Storm-racked islands, glaciers, and forests that came down together to the sea formed the setting of one of the last great untraveled regions of the world.

These years of speculation preceded a journey that in many ways only added enchantment to that distant land. It began in the late summer of 1972. I journeyed south through Argentina to take passage on a ship that was to sail from Punta Arenas on the Strait of Magellan. Crossing the Negro River which, east of the Andes, forms the northern limit of Patagonia, I passed through the open steppelike country that runs for nearly a thousand miles south to the strait. It was dry, with long ravines scarring the countryside and a ragged covering of coarse grasses and scrub. I came to know it as a land of clear skies and keen winds. Nearer the mountains and across the border into Chile (the frontier here curls eastward to Cape Virgins on the Atlantic), the country became greener. Stretches of forest appeared and then, not far from Punta Arenas, I was among the foothills of the Andes. Sloping gently at first, they ran into higher peaks, many with traces of winter snow and their tops hidden in swirling mist.

Capital of the Chilean province of Magallanes, Punta

Punta Arenas, Chile's capital of the south and commercial center on the Strait of Magellan

Arenas (meaning Sandy Point) grew up as the commercial center of the large sheep-farming estates, or estancias, of southern Patagonia. For many years it enjoyed the prestige of being the main port of call and fueling station on the sea passage between the Atlantic and Pacific oceans. Any ship going, say, from Boston to San Francisco would normally come to Punta Arenas unless it risked the stormy passage around Cape Horn. In 1912, Punta Arenas' fortunes changed with the opening of the Panama Canal. Fewer and fewer ships came south and but for the timely development of new industries, Punta Arenas might have sunk into the obscurity of a small coastal town at the far south of the inhabited world.

The day I sailed from Punta Arenas it was as if the town were poised on the edge of spring. One sensed that there the two faces of Patagonia—the wet and the dry—came together. Leaving the sunshine and open skies behind, I entered a dark and rather forbidding world. The surging sea and a desolate coast slipped by in an ever-changing pattern of mists. To the west, barely a mile away, lay the coast of the Brunswick Peninsula, and there I caught glimpses of the mountains that have played such a profound part in shaping the climate of this region.

The Andes follow the Pacific coast for nearly five thousand miles, forming the high backbone of South America. In the south, beyond the province of Chiloé (the northern limit of the Chilean part of Patagonia), they are a bleak world of ice and rock, crossed by deep forested valleys and narrow arms of the sea. Little explored in many parts, the frontier between Argentina and Chile lies along the crest of these mountains, for much of its length from five to ten thousand feet above sea level. Strong damp winds blow in from the west, and as they rise over the land the moisture in them conden-

Narrow arms of the sea thread the mountainous Pacific coast of Patagonia dividing it into a maze of rocky islands and headlands.

ses as rain and snow, making the Pacific side of Patagonia one of the stormiest and wettest regions on Earth.

Beyond the Strait of Magellan the Andes curl to the southeast, crossing the archipelago of Tierra del Fuego and dipping finally under the sea at Staten Island. This legendary archipelago, usually considered to be a part of Patagonia, is a continuation of the giant fretwork of submerged mountains and narrow seas that characterize the southern Pacific coast of the continent. Only in the east, on the island known as Isla Grande, are there open expanses similar to the Argentinian steppe to the north of the strait. For the rest, Tierra del Fuego is a chain of rugged islands, with the famous promontory of Cape Horn at its tip.

14

Until the mid-eighteen hundreds there had been very little interest in these cold windswept lands of the far south. Apart from a handful of isolated settlements on the coasts, the only inhabitants were groups of primitive nomadic Indians. Far more interest, in fact, had centered on the stormy cape that dominated the deep-sea passage between the Old World and the Pacific. Tales of the ships and men that rounded The Horn in the days of sail have provided some of the most stirring epics in the history of the sea. This era drew to a close with the coming of steam, when vessels could take the sheltered and far safer route through the Strait of Magellan. In 1843 the coasts alongside the strait came under Chilean sovereignty and shortly afterward Punta Arenas was founded.

During my own voyage, in the comfort and safety of a Chilean naval ship, I was constantly reminded of the feats and hazards of former days. Soon after leaving Punta Arenas two low headlands appeared across the strait. They marked

Strong winds blow across the southern tip of the continent, shaping trees and keeping most of the life down in the shelter of valleys.

the entrance to Bahía Inútil (Useless Bay)—a deep cul-de-sac that frustrated an early attempt to find a way to the open sea. On the other side of the strait lay Port Famine, a deserted tree-fringed bay and site of an early tragic attempt by Spain to plant a colony in the region. Other names followed on the map, names that told of the hopes and fears of the navigators of old—Cape Desolation, Anxious Point, East and West Furies, Last Hope Inlet.

Rounding Cape Froward, the ship took a more westerly course toward the Pacific. Mountains came down close on either side, looming darkly over the narrow lead of water of the strait. It was a dismal scene, for the clouds hung low and the rain came in gray streaming shafts. Sometimes an albatross flew alongside for a moment, and then swept away on stiff wings low over the waves.

The western end of Magellan's Strait is marked by three rocky islets called The Evangelists, where there is a lighthouse. Lying directly in the path of the southern circumpolar winds, the seas there are among the wildest and most turbulent in the world. Waves are whipped up to fifty feet or more in height, and one can imagine the lonely vigil of lighthouse keepers marooned sometimes for weeks on end in their sea-lashed beacon. It is said that a relief ship once waited forty days at a nearby anchorage for the weather to improve and the chance to make a landing. The anchorage is known to this day as Cuarenta Días (Forty Days).

To avoid the heavy seas most ships turn into the Smyth Channel before reaching The Evangelists. A remarkable series of channels leads northward and through these ocean-going ships can travel most of the way to Puerto Montt, an important sea- and rail-terminal to the north of Chiloé. The main route is marked by fixed navigation lights, but it is a

16

long tortuous passage which even modern vessels take three or four days to complete. The tops of mountains emerge on all sides and miniature icebergs, calved from the glaciers, drift along with the tides—a delight to visitors and never-failing hazard to shipping. The journey has been called a voyage through the Andes and it is difficult to think of a more apt description.

For me they were pleasant days because there was so much that was new and I was fortunate in that my Navy hosts had a schedule which involved visiting several remote places off the main navigation channel. For a week we threaded narrow arms of the sea, only once—in crossing the Gulf of Peñas and rounding the Taitao Peninsula—coming out into the open Pacific.

The first night the ship anchored by low wooded islands off

Servicing fixed navigation lights in the Smyth Channel

the coast of the Muñoz Gamero Peninsula. In the morning the clouds parted and I had my first glimpse of the haunting beauty of this region. The mirror-calm sea and nearby slopes were bathed in sunlight. The clouds, even as they cleared, were suffused with soft pastel colors which matched the tranquility of the scene. Many waterfowl, as if they too had been affected by the magic of the day, suddenly appeared; and far over the glassy stillness I could see small groups of ducks, cormorants, and even penguins. A little later the clear jagged peaks of an isolated volcano, Mount Burney, rose above the forest. Its high snow-covered summit stood like a crystal above the great blue-veined glaciers that tumbled down its sides. Almost as we weighed anchor and got underway a blanket of cloud swept around and hid these wonders as effectively as night. I decided then that one day I would return to see more of this land. Little could I have known that the following year chance would again bring me to those shores, to spend a month among the glaciers and forests of that strange mountain.

The forests fringing the coast of this part of Patagonia, and the northerly provinces of Aisén and Chiloé, are composed largely of southern or false beeches. There are several species, similar to our beeches of the northern hemisphere, but noticeably different in the rougher bark and usually much smaller leaves, which are clustered together more closely on the twigs. What is particularly interesting about these trees is that they also grow in New Zealand and other far-off regions of the southern Pacific. This rather curious distribution is explained by the theory of an ancient landmass linking at

Opposite: *Southern beeches near Port Famine on the Strait of Magellan*

18

one time Patagonia, Antarctica, and New Zealand. The southern beeches at that early period of the Earth's history must have had a far wider range over the southern parts of the world; and their occurrence today in such diverse places as Patagonia and the New Zealand Alps is striking botanical evidence in support of the theory of a Southern Continent.

Forests of beech follow the coast of the Muñoz Gamero Peninsula round to the north, where an arm of the sea links the Smyth Channel with Ultima Esperanza (Last Hope) Inlet. It was in a cave above the tree-clad slopes of the Last Hope Inlet that there was made, at the end of the last century, one of the most exciting discoveries relating to the early prehistory of Patagonia.

For many years the fossilized remains of giant animals had intrigued visitors to Patagonia. They had been found at many places on the dry eastern side of the Andes and, together with petrified forests, seemed to indicate that humid conditions were formerly much more extensive. Among the strangest of these animals were glyptodons and ground sloths. The glyptodons were giant grazing animals related to the armadillos. They must have looked like the legendary monsters of medieval times, for they had rigid shells eight or nine feet long, bony shields on their heads, and tails heavily armed with knobs and spines. The ground sloths were even more bulky, one species being at least the size of an elephant. One can imagine the rather awesome spectacle of these huge beasts shuffling around and rearing up on their hind legs to claw down the branches of trees for food. Other strange herbivores, with long necks, were related to the camels. Perhaps the most intriguing thing of all about these Patagonian giants is that they appear to have been still around when man arrived on the scene.

20

In 1895 a German sea captain, Hermann Eberhardt, exploring the cave at Ultima Esperanza, came upon some giant bones. These were taken back to be examined by experts and proved sufficiently interesting for further searches to be made. A piece of hide was then discovered beneath a mantle of powdered rock, and attached to the skin were hair and muscles. Embedded in the inner side were curious bean-shaped nodules of bone which made the hide, in effect, a cross between a fur coat and a suit of armor. From these and other remains a kind of ground sloth, called mylodon, was described. Further searches in the area revealed a cave with piles of cut hay, a rough enclosure walled off at one end, and more remains of animals. These latest finds suggested that some of the giants had either been trapped or kept there in a state of semi-domestication.

Cave of the mylodon near Last Hope Inlet

The discovery attracted the interest of such famous scientists of the day as Florentino Ameghino, the Argentinian paleontologist, and Professor E. Ray Lancaster, the director of the British Museum of Natural History, who thought it possible that giant ground sloths might still exist in some remote unexplored part of Patagonia. Several expeditions were mounted specifically to search for the animals and to see if one could be captured alive. Although no dramatic discoveries were made, and no hope now remains of finding a mylodon alive, further strange facts did come to light. One of these was that the huge shells of glyptodons had been used as roofing material by early man in Patagonia. Furthermore, certain legends of the local Indians seemed to point to the idea that their ancestors had been familiar with giant animals and that these animals had later disappeared. The story of these vanished giants provides one of the strangest and most exciting chapters in the history of Patagonia.

2

Early Peoples

Dating studies on remains of the giant sloth found in the Mylodon Cave placed their age at around 9,000 B.C. The remarkable state of preservation of the piece of skin was due to the dryness of the cave and possibly the deposits of fine powdered rock which had provided a cap excluding the corrosive effects of the atmosphere.

These finds date back to about the time of man's first appearance in Patagonia. He made his way from the north, attracted by the abundance of game that thrived along the edges of the mountains and forests. No doubt, even then, the ground sloths and glyptodons were on the decline. All through prehistory successive groups of animals have thrived and, in turn, faded away as conditions became less favorable to their existence. In the case of the Patagonian giants, a combination of factors must have been responsible for their disappearance. Climatic changes seem to have been one of them, for it is now believed that prolonged droughts resulted in forage becoming scarcer. The competition of newly-arrived species from the north, and the diseases they brought, may have been decisive in a number of cases. Finally, man himself, with his specialized hunting techniques, must have hastened the extinction of some of these ponderous giants. The huge armor-encased glyptodons, for instance, were fairly safe until the new two-legged invader came along who could throw stones and kindle fire.

These first hunters were followed by other waves of immigrants. We know little about these people, apart from what can be deduced from implements of chipped stone and paintings and etchings left behind on suitable rock faces. Their lives, in any event, were dominated by the chase. In the

The open treeless plains of eastern Patagonia were the home of the nomadic Patagones or Tehuelche Indians.

unending quest for food, these early men must have been continually on the move. Well before the first Europeans appeared on the scene in the sixteenth century, some divergence had occurred—between one nomadic group who were inhabitants of the open plains and another group who sought a livelihood along the coastal waterways as gatherers of seafoods.

It seems likely that these two groups arrived independently of each other, traveling down on either side of the Andes, which in the south form an almost continuous barrier to the movement of people on foot. The plains-dwellers probably arrived first, for traveling there was easier, and we know that early man had reached the Strait of Magellan some eleven thousand years ago.

The people of the canals and waterways of the Pacific and Fuegan coasts are known as the canoe-Indians. They are subdivided into the Chonos, the Alacalufs, and the Yahgans (or Yamanas). On the plains, two main groups of hunters, or foot-Indians, were the Patagones and the Onas (or Shelknam). Each of these groups, or linguistic families, had its own characteristic dialects and customs.

The word "Patagonia" is derived from *Tierra de Patagones*, Land of the Big-feet, a name recorded by Antonio Pigafetta, chronicler of Magellan's famous voyage of discovery, when giant footprints were discovered near their winter camp at San Julián in 1520. Pigafetta and later travelers described the Patagones in colorful terms and the legend persisted that the Indians were giants of mankind. It seems that their size was exaggerated by their clothes—high conical hats and voluminous robes of fur, which they wore as a protection against the cold winds. They also used moccasins and leggings of animal skins, and it is not surprising that the large prints of these

25

hides stretched over their feet astonished visitors who came across them.

The Patagones, or Tehuelches as they are better known, roamed over a territory that corresponds today to the greater part of Argentinian Patagonia and the very south of mainland Chile. The banks of the Negro River formed the boundary in the north, and in the south they reached the Strait of Magellan. The principal animal that provided them with food and clothing was the guanaco, a member of the camel family which ranges widely over the southern plains of South America. The association, in fact, between man and beast was comparable with that of the more familiar one between Eskimo and caribou. Guanacos and other game were hunted with bolas—a curious invention in which two or three rounded stones, encased in leather and joined by thongs, were hurled to entangle the legs and bring down the quarry. Rheas (flightless ostrichlike birds), armadillos, skunks, and shellfish all contributed to the diet of the Tehuelches; and at certain seasons they gathered the fruits of barberry and wild currants. Their homes were made from the stitched hides of the guanaco spread over a framework of branches—light shelters which could be carried easily from place to place as their owners moved over the trackless plains of Patagonia.

In the north, the territory of the Tehuelches bordered that of the Araucanian Indians. It was from this latter tribe or the nearby Puelches that horses, brought originally by the Spaniards to the River Plate, found their way to the Tehuelches. By the middle of the eighteenth century many of them had

Opposite: *The guanaco, a humpless member of the camel family, supplied the foot-Indians with food and clothing.*

become mounted nomads, riding with great skill and using lassos, lances, and bolas on horseback.

The Ona Indians lived in the interior of the main island of Tierra del Fuego. They were a branch of the Tehuelches and most probably came from the northern tribe at a time when a way existed across what is now the Strait of Magellan. (The eastern part of the strait is a geological displacement, or faultline, believed to have been formed in the last few thousand years.) The Onas were a race of tall, rather noble, people who hunted the guanaco with bows and arrows. Like the Tehuelches, they were wonderfully skillful at making arrows, chipping the heads from pieces of flint and rock crystal, and fastening these to shafts of forest barberry. Small molelike rodents, called tucotucos, were also hunted for food, especially by the northern Onas. The animals were speared in their underground burrows with pointed stakes, and their meat was roasted on hot embers. Fire, which was very important to the Indians, was made by striking pyrites on a rock to produce a spark which kindled strips of dried puffball (a kind of large spherical fungus) used as tinder.

One group about whom we know very little was the Haush, a Fuegan foot-tribe, related to the Onas, who inhabited the Mitre Peninsula in the mountainous southeastern tip of Isla Grande. As the Onas themselves asserted, when speaking to the early missionaries, the Haush were a distinct tribe with their own dialect and customs. They were seen by Europeans as early as 1619, but the inhospitable nature of the coastal swamps and forests of the Mitre Peninsula forbade almost any contact with them.

The neighbors of the Onas along the coasts and waterways of Tierra del Fuego were the Yahgans. The southernmost inhabitants of the world, they were a hardy race whose indif-

Ona Indians of Tierra del Fuego clad in guanaco skin robes. This photograph was taken at the beginning of this century, when the tribe was already sadly reduced in numbers.

Pan del Indio (Indian's bread) are fungi which grow on the southern beeches. Also known as tree morels, they were collected for food by the Onas of Tierra del Fuego.

Ona Indian woman, child, and their home

ference to the bitter climate amazed early explorers. Some went about naked, while at best a sea otter pelt or seal skin draped over the shoulders and another small piece worn about the loins gave little protection against the winds and cold of the Fuegan winter, with temperatures around freezing. Essentially wanderers, they traveled in canoes, feeding on shellfish and whatever else they found along the shores: birds and eggs, seals, fish, crabs, and an occasional whale or porpoise stranded by the tide. Certain plants, such as a celery, which grew along the beaches, a kind of cress, and the young shoots of tussock grass, gave a little variety to this fare. One thing that the Yahgans were very careful about was to keep a fire going. Even when they were on the move they guarded smouldering pieces of green wood on a bed of clay or upturned turf in their canoes.

The canoe-Indians were smaller in stature than the Onas and the Tehuelches. Besides being rather squat, the physical appearance generally of the Yahgans evidently left much to be desired—at least to European eyes. Nineteenth century travelers spoke of their savage and "villainous" expressions— broad features, matted hair, greasy copper-colored skin, and eyes (no doubt through sitting too long over their fires) very red and sore-looking. The naturalist Charles Darwin wrote that he could hardly believe that they were fellow creatures and inhabitants of the same world. Yet, the Yahgans lived in one of the harshest of environments, and in many ways they were peculiarly successful. One dour and unpleasant task performed by the women was to tie up the canoes among the rafts of giant seaweeds that fringe the coasts and then swim ashore through the icy water—a dangerous undertaking; the men, apparently, could not, or would not, swim.

Like the Yahgans, the Alacalufs of the western channels were a hardy group of canoe-Indians. Their territory stretched from Magellan's Strait northward to the Gulf of Peñas. As the American anthropologist Junius Bird pointed out, three things made life bearable for them: the beech trees which provided bark for their canoes, the wood of *tepú* for fires, and the abundant shellfish which were their principal food. Families tended to use the same campsites year after year and, as a result, vast heaps of mussel shells accumulated from their meals. Some of these deposits, or middens, examined by anthropologists have been as much as thirteen feet deep. Their homes were simple wigwams of boughs, bent over at the top and covered with green branches, fern fronds, bark, and skins. An open fire was built in the center of the hut, the smoke escaping through the open top. None of these tribes

31

had cooking pots and food, when it was cooked, was simply roasted in the flames or on hot embers.

A census by the Chilean authorities in 1971 recorded only 47 surviving Alacalufs. Some of these were of mixed descent, and all but three lived at the settlement of Puerto Edén on the coast of Wellington Island. It is an open question as to whether or not the Alacalufs (or any of the other Indian groups) can still be identified as a distinct tribe. Their use of the Spanish language, European clothes, and increasing contacts with outsiders are all drawing the remnant into the gen-

Beds of giant kelp, some of the plants growing into great tangles many hundreds of feet in length, ring the coasts of southern Patagonia.

Forest-fringed bay of Puerto Muñoz Gamero, former haunt of the
Alacaluf Indians. Remains of their shellfish middens are scattered along
the shore.

eral mixed-blooded population of southern Chile.

The Chonos have gone already. They lived to the north of
the Alacalufs, along a 300-mile stretch of coast carved by the
sea into a maze of thickly-wooded islands and headlands.
What little we know of their existence comes from the writ-
ings of navigators and Jesuit missionaries of the seventeenth
and eighteenth centuries. Their territory lay far enough north
for limited agriculture to be possible—although it was little
practiced by the Chonos. Potatoes, which they must have
acquired originally from their northern neighbors, were

33

grown in small quantities; otherwise, their lives could not have been so different from those of the other canoe-Indians. The Chonos must always have been a small group, and it is now a hundred years since anything has been seen or heard of them.

To the north of the Chonos, on the island of Chiloé, lived people who had a more highly developed life and culture and who, properly speaking, belonged to the tribes of central Chile. As such, they are not generally considered as being among the early people of Patagonia. Chiloé, in any case, has a history of European settlement going back to the sixteenth century, and the traditional life of its indigenous Indians was lost at an early date.

The tragic fact today is that virtually all the early peoples of Patagonia have disappeared. The Alacalufs are down to seven or eight families, the Yahgans number no more than half a dozen individuals (in Chilean Tierra del Fuego), and if any purebred Onas survive they are very old people. The native tongues, when they are spoken at all, have been mutilated by the introduction of Spanish words and phrases. The legendary Tehuelches, the most warlike and numerous of the early tribes, were swept away during a series of bitter struggles in the 1880s following the European settlement of the Patagonian plains. Although a small colony of Tehuelches lives in an Argentinian government reservation at Camusú Aike in the province of Santa Cruz, they are represented by half-castes and people whose lives—like the Chilotes'—are very different from those of their ancestors.

The reasons for the disappearance of these tribes are all related in one way or another to the arrival of white man. As the mylodon went before them, so these early people have been superceded by invaders who were more ruthless and better adapted to survive in changing times. The analogy, of course, is not a strict one, for the newcomers possessed a sense of reasoning, and a closer contact could have been developed between the old and the new inhabitants.

Early encounters with both the canoe- and the foot-Indians revealed a friendliness toward outsiders. Instances are recorded when they gave food and shelter to people shipwrecked on their shores. For many years the Tehuelches traded with white settlers in the south, the Indians bringing guanaco meat and skins to exchange for beads, tobacco,

The Onas hunted guanaco along the northern forest fringes of Isla Grande in Tierra del Fuego.

sugar, ammunition, and rum. George Musters, who traveled among the Tehuelches in 1869, spoke of the intelligence and generous disposition of the Indians, but noticed that they were already beginning to suffer from the insidious effects of liquor. Confidence turned to distrust when designs of the white invaders became apparent, and a series of feuds and misunderstandings quickly made matters worse. In 1872 sheep ranchers began to seize land in Tierra del Fuego and there followed a ruthless campaign to exterminate the Onas. The struggle was terribly one-sided and it was not long before the Fuegans, like the Tehuelches, had disappeared from very many of their former haunts.

Added to these bitter events there came another and worse hazard. The natives had little or no natural immunity to diseases brought, inadvertently, by settlers. Respiratory ailments, epidemics of measles, typhoid, whooping cough, and smallpox all made fatal inroads into the fast dwindling populations. Many Onas were simply left to die so that their lands could be taken. In thirty years their numbers fell from some 3,500 to only 350. In 1950 forty people said to be Onas remained, but the majority of these were of mixed blood and all were employed as workers on sheep farms.

Early missionaries working among the Indians met with little success; and, indeed, it must remain doubtful if the implanting of Christian ideals could have had much benefit or meaning during those confused and lawless years. Certainly, in some ways, trying to change the beliefs of the Indians only hastened the break-up of the tribes, and the work of the missionaries has been criticized on those grounds. At the same time the missionaries were among the very few people who were prepared to help the Indian and to speak on his behalf

36

in the face of all the exploitation going on around him. It is also important to remember the changing attitudes of the times. At the end of the last century no one would have dreamed of looking at the Yahgans and Onas as the end products of a specialized, if simple, way of life in which self-confidence and an integrated code of behavior and customs were essential for their well-being in a hostile environment. The new science of anthropology had hardly begun and problems were seen in quite a different light.

The day to day life of these Stone Age peoples was deeper and more complex than might be imagined. Elaborate rituals were an important part of tribal life which knitted together different family groups. Among the Onas, the shamans or medicine men were the guardians of the tribe's traditions. Languages were rich and expressive. A remarkable dictionary of the Yahgan language, compiled by Thomas Bridges, a pastor of the Patagonian Missionary Society, contains no fewer than 32,000 words and inflections. From this we gain a unique insight into the customs and linguistics of these Indians. During the present century several anthropologists, notably Martin Gusinde and Junius Bird, have made further valuable contributions to our knowledge of these lost and vanishing civilizations.

It is incredible how recently all these events took place. Thoughts of the Yahgans were brought to me vividly and sadly one evening on the Beagle Channel in Tierra del Fuego. I went down to a beach used by the Indians when they came ashore for their camps. The scene and setting would have been so familiar to them: the snow-flecked hills of Navarino Island across the strait, low wooded headlands, and the distant calls of wild geese. I expected at almost any moment to see a family of Yahgans coming in—black tousled heads peering over the edge of their canoe and a wisp of smoke drifting across the water. On the ground by me, barely covered by grass, were the heaps of mussel shells, mixed with ash and bones of fish, that remained from their meals. It was almost as if the owners had gone away for the summer and as the antarctic beeches turned color so they would return to their winter haunts. Alas, the world is a poorer place because these people have left us.

3

The First Explorers

The discovery of Patagonia resulted from searches for a sea passage that would link Europe and the East. Trade with the Moluccas, the famous "Isles of Spice" of the East Indies, had attracted the rival attentions of Spain and Portugal and led to the quest for a new way round the lands discovered by Columbus.

In 1519 the Portuguese navigator Hernando de Magallanes (known in English as Ferdinand Magellan), then in the service of Spain, sailed from the port of San Lúcar de Barrameda bound for the New World. Arguing by analogy of the African continent, the southern tip of which he had rounded on previous voyages, Magellan believed that a way would lie to the south of the American continent. Crossing the Atlantic, his little fleet of five ships (the largest 120 tons) reached the estuary of the River Plate and from there made its way to the south, hugging the coast and keeping a constant lookout for a passage to the west. Among the many new and strange things Magellan and his companions saw were elephant seals, huge beasts that sprawled upon the beaches, and flightless birds that were later to be called penguins. In April, 1520,

with the southern winter approaching, the fleet anchored in a tiny harbor surrounded by low hills. It was a bleak spot, with hardly any vegetation beyond stunted wind-torn scrub, but at least it was somewhere sheltered to pass the winter. It was at this place, known today as San Julián, that the first contact by Europeans was made with the Patagones or Tehuelche Indians.

In August, with winter behind them, Magellan's fleet continued sailing to the south. Eight weeks later they found a passage leading to the west. The ebb and flow of the tide and movements of the currents suggested to Magellan that a channel would lead through to a far sea; they entered and sailed through the 330-mile strait that was later to bear the great navigator's name.

Magellan's voyage has become one of the most famous epics of discovery of all time. Few persons, before or since, have reached further into the unknown. His ships were the first to cross the southern sea, which Magellan named the Pacific, and to circumnavigate the globe. But perhaps the most spectacular discovery of this remarkable voyage was the strait that carved its way through the rugged tip of South America.

Magellan had no way of knowing what lay beyond the strait to the south. It might have been part of a huge landmass. There were people there, for he had seen fires along the shore and had called the land Tierra del Fuego (Land of Fire). Other navigators followed. Six years later Frey García Jofré de Loayza passed through Magellan's Strait and reached the Moluccas. But it was not until the voyage of the

Opposite: *Statue of Magellan at Punta Arenas*

English seaman Francis Drake that it was realized that Tierra del Fuego was a group of islands.

With the voyage of Drake, the rivalries of Spain and England were carried into the Pacific. It is against this background that we must view many of the events of the next two centuries.

Drake, with the title of Captain General, sailed from the England of Queen Elizabeth I in 1577 bound for the South Seas. Five well-armed ships, including the *Pelican* (later to be renamed *Golden Hind*), and some 164 seamen and adventurers made up the expedition. Nine months out of Plymouth the fleet passed Cape Virgins and sailed into the Strait of Magellan. In two weeks they were through to the Pacific . . . but then the weather turned and Drake and his companions were swept back to the southeast. For seven weeks they struggled against the winds and heavy seas, being driven toward the Antarctic to discover that part of the southern sea which runs past Cape Horn. The longitude they reached had already been approached by ships from the east, and from this Drake surmised that open sea must lie all around the southern tip of the continent. When the fleet could finally make headway and sail northward along the western coast of Patagonia it was to spring a surprise on the Spaniards. Drake's sudden appearance on the rich and unprotected coast of New Spain did little to please King Philip II who straightaway resolved to bar the passage to the Pacific to all but the ships of Spain.

To guard the strait, however, was a far from easy matter. Thought had already been given to this forty years before when the Portuguese knight Simón de Alcazaba had been granted a concession to establish a settlement there. The expedition had been ill-fated from the beginning, being

42

Shingle beaches of south Patagonia where a forty-foot tide runs.

driven by storms on to the coast north of San Julián where its leader had been murdered by mutineers. A year later, Emperor Charles V of Spain authorized Francisco de Camargo to make an attempt to set up a Strait Province. This grandiose scheme, involving a territory stretching all the way north to the modern province of Buenos Aires, foundered when Camargo's flagship ran aground near Cape Virgins. The voyage of Juan de Ladrillero, 1557–59, did little to restore confidence. After a voyage of exploration, during which he had taken formal possession of Magellan's Strait and its

43

shores in the name of the Spanish governor of New Extrema-dura (the territory of this colony had been extended to include the strait in 1554), Ladrillero had been overtaken by misfortune. Running out of supplies, members of his crew died one after another, and when finally their home port of Concepción (today a part of Chile) was reached only Ladrillero and two companions were still alive; and they too soon died.

There then followed Spain's most famous and tragic attempt to colonize the Strait of Magellan. The viceroy of Peru, don Francisco Toledo, sent two ships under the command of Pedro Sarmiento de Gamboa to look into ways of thwarting any recurrence of Drake's adventures. Sailing from Callao a year after the English corsairs had swept up the coast, Sarmiento made a remarkable voyage of discovery, carefully and accurately charting the channels and strait and finally deciding that the latter could be fortified by planting a settlement on the shores of its eastern section. He continued his voyage across the Atlantic to report directly to the king and the Royal Council of the Indies in Spain.

King Philip was sufficiently impressed with Sarmiento and his plans to assemble the largest fleet ever to be sent to America. In 1581, 23 ships with over 3,000 people on board sailed from San Lúcar, the same port from which Magellan had departed a little over half a century before. Diego Flores de Valdés had been appointed commander of the expedition and Sarmiento had the title of Governor and Captain General of Magellan's Strait. Their object was to found a colony that would be in a position to close the passage to the Pacific and thereby protect the coasts of Chile and Peru from privateers. Had Sarmiento known of Drake's discovery of the way round to the south of Tierra del Fuego (which had been guarded

44

as a state secret by the British admiralty), he would have realized how futile was his task and saved untold misery.

Troubles began almost from the outset. Flores de Valdés was not a happy choice as commander, and this was to lead to mutiny and desertions. Before leaving Europe, the fleet was crippled by the loss of five ships in a storm and had to put in to Cádiz for refitting and to replenish supplies. When, over two years later, they entered the Strait of Magellan the magnificent expedition had been reduced to five ships and a bare 500 men and women. Undeterred, Sarmiento founded the first settlement, which he called Nombre de Jesús, on the coast a little to the southwest of Cape Virgins. The date was February 11, 1584.

The three best ships then deserted, leaving the unfortunate Sarmiento and 350 people to brave the winter on the wild Patagonian coast. Their provisions were inadequate and they had scarcely any tools with which to construct the new settlement. Of the two ships that remained, one was unseaworthy and the other, a small caravel, called the *Santa María*, had been left virtually stripped of her running tackle and supplies. Furthermore, the Tehuelche Indians, who came several times to their camp, showed evident signs of becoming unfriendly. As desperate as the situation appeared, Sarmiento sent the *Santa María* along the coast to a site for the main settlement which he had noticed on the outward journey from Callao. Leaving the others to commence building and to sow crops in the more sheltered spots they could find, he and 95 others marched overland to found the City of Rey don Felipe (King Philip) on the shore of the little bay where they rejoined the *Santa María*.

One cannot really think of less auspicious circumstances for the founding of a city. Sarmiento appointed from his followers the future authorities, laid out sites for the plaza and principal buildings, and watched the stone foundations of the little church rise on a hill above the bay. Then fate turned an even crueler hand. Winter came early and with it the cold antarctic weather which sweeps up from the south. After a series of dreadful misfortunes, during which Sarmiento tried desperately to bring help to his marooned settlements, the little colony suffered the extreme agonies of a slow death from cold and starvation.

In the summer of 1587, a squadron of three ships flying the English flag and commanded by Thomas Cavendish came to anchor in the bay by the City of King Philip. On board was Tomás Hernández, who had been rescued by Cavendish, a lone survivor of the heroic colonizing adventure of Sarmiento. The aspect of the abandoned city, where everyone had died, so appalled the English seamen that they called it Port Famine.

The growth of England, France, and Holland as trading nations brought increased activity to the region of the strait. Although attempts at fortifying the passage to the west ended with Sarmiento, the whole area remained a considerable thorn in the side of Spain. She was far from having complete command of the seas and at the same time was desirous of keeping to herself a monopoly of commerce with her American colonies. Following Drake and Cavendish, other adventurers appeared to harass the Spanish fleets and to seek trade in the Pacific. Among these were Andrew Merrick, John Davis, and Richard Hawkins—all protagonists of the growing hostility between Spain and England—and the Dutchmen, Simon de Cordes and Olivier van Noort.

In 1616 the Dutch discovered Cape Horn. Holland at that time had strict trading laws and, as these limited the use of

Elephant seals, valued for their high quality oil, were killed by many early visitors to the coasts of Patagonia.

Early voyagers spoke of the huge penguin colonies and of the importance of these birds in provisioning ships.

the Cape of Good Hope and Magellan's Strait to ships of the influential Dutch East India Company, it became all the more imperative for private companies to find another way to the East. With this in mind, a wealthy Antwerp trader, Isaac Le Maire, sent Willem Schouten to explore to the south of Magellan's Strait. Le Maire believed that open sea would lie beyond Tierra del Fuego. Captain Schouten rounded the headland, later named Cape Horn (after his home town of Hoorn), and sailed to the west, so proving in practical terms the earlier predictions of Drake. The voyage became one of the greatest of private exploring enterprises.

The quest for geographical knowledge led to a series of exploratory and scientific expeditions. These continued through the seventeenth, eighteenth, and nineteenth centuries and helped to build a coherent picture of the lands at the southern tip of America.

Following the expedition of Schouten and Le Maire, the Nodal brothers of Spain surveyed the Strait of Magellan and eastern Tierra del Fuego—where they were the first Europeans to come across the Haush Indians. Later came the voyages of John Narborough, William Dampier, Woodes Rogers, and John Clipperton, those of the Frenchmen Gennes and Beauchesne, and many others. All these added valuable information about the inhabitants, climate, hydrography, and resources of the region. Narborough questioned the idea that the Patagonian Indians were a race of giants, for the tallest he found measured just under six feet. A Jesuit priest, Nicolás Mascardi, made several remarkable journeys across the interior of Patagonia during the years 1670–73, in part to search for the legendary "City of the Caesars." Reports of a mysterious city, inhabited by Spanish-speaking people, had been linked with the fabulous riches of the temples and palaces

Cape Horn

of the Incas. Whatever was the source of the rumors—perhaps a small settlement of survivors from Sarmiento's City of King Philip—they were nurtured by the wildly romantic spirit of the times.

The period 1681–1720 brought the expeditions of the buccaneers. It was another ruthless and colorful era with seamen of France, Holland, and England, linked by a common hatred they professed for Spain, engaged in piracy and illicit commerce with her colonies. To the names of Beauchesne, Dampier, Rogers, and Clipperton, there are now added Bartholomew Sharp, Edward Davis, and Ambrose Cowley. These, and many others, found a refuge and a base for their activities among the intricate channels of the coasts of Patagonia. This period will always be associated with the Golden Age of sail, with the legends of Cape Horn and that dreaded ensign—the black flag with the Death's Head in white.

As if these will-o'-the-wisp activities of the pirates were not trouble enough for Spain, there came repeated rumors of settlements by her enemies around the coast of Patagonia. The Dutchman Cordes had spent a suspiciously long time prospecting around the Strait of Magellan; and then stories kept filtering through from the Indians that the English had established a base somewhere in the unexplored lands of the south. Expeditions by Bartolomé Días Gallardo, Antonio de Vea and, later, Cosme Ugarte were all sent to check the truth of these rumors.

By 1740 Spain and England were actually at war and in that year the British admiralty sent a fleet of warships under Lord Anson to upset the commerce of Spain with her colonies. Both Anson's fleet and that of the Spanish admiral, José Alfonso Pizarro, who had been sent to intercept him, ran into violent storms off Cape Horn. The conditions not only prevented the two sides from meeting but broke up both fleets and many ships were lost. One, *H.M.S. Wager*, was wrecked on an island near the Gulf of Peñas and to this day the island is known as Wager Island.

On board the *Wager* when she was wrecked was John Byron, grandfather of the poet Lord Byron, who was later to make a second voyage around the coasts of Patagonia. The expeditions of Commodore Byron, his countryman James Cook, the distinguished French explorer Louis Antoine de Bougainville, and those of the Spaniard Antonio Córdoba Laso de la Vega and Alejandro Malaspina—an Italian in the service of the Spanish crown—all continued the growing tradition of geographical exploration.

An interesting voyage of this time was the forerunner of several commissioned by Jesuit missionaries of the Island of Chiloé. In 1766 José García, with three large planked canoes, was sent to work among the Indians inhabiting the southern canals. It will be remembered that the one exposed point on the voyage south is round the Taitao Peninsula, where ships have to venture into the open Pacific. Since times immemorial the Alacalufs and Chonos had known of a low marshy strip of land between two arms of the sea, over which canoes could be carried and so avoid this dangerous passage. It was over this neck of land, the Isthmus of Ofqui, that García now took his three boats. The route was used on a number of subsequent occasions to transport the small vessels of the missionaries.

In the late 1700s, new attempts to colonize Patagonia were made by the government of Spain. Juan de la Piedra founded the port of San José on the Valdés Peninsula, but it survived only until 1810 when it was destroyed by the Indians. Ex-

The face of Patagonia has been moulded by the climate and strong winds; above, Lake Argentino, the source of the Santa Cruz River.

peditions under Antonio Viedma and others were sent to San Julián and the Santa Cruz River and, although they achieved no immediate results, small trading posts were established, and these formed the basis of settlements which came a century later.

The Wars of Independence from Spain put an end temporarily to the voyages of discovery. With the restoration of peace, new emphasis was given to the charting of the southern coasts of South America. Two of the most famous names connected with the survey of Patagonia and Tierra del Fuego are Philip Parker King and Robert FitzRoy.

In 1826 two hydrographic vessels of the British Navy, *Adventure* and *Beagle*, began a systematic survey of the coasts. The task was to take nearly ten years. The commander of the expedition and captain of the *Adventure* for the first part of the survey, which lasted four years, was King. Halfway through this period the captaincy of *H.M.S. Beagle* passed to a young flag lieutenant named Robert FitzRoy.

On his return to England in 1830, FitzRoy took with him on the *Beagle* four Yahgan Indians from Tierra del Fuego. They were given the rather strange names of Boat Memory, Fuegia Basket, Jemmy Button, and York Minster. Boat Memory died from smallpox shortly after reaching England, but the other three were vaccinated in time and soon settled down to receive the benefits of a formal education. They were lodged at FitzRoy's expense in the house of a clergyman near London where they were taught English and such useful crafts as carpentry and gardening. During the year or so they spent in England, the three young Fuegans were objects of great interest, being presented toward the end of their stay to the king and queen at St. James's Palace. Queen Adelaide seems to have been much taken with Fuegia and gave her a bonnet and a ring.

The second expedition to Patagonia consisted only of *Beagle* under the command of Captain FitzRoy. On board, with the three returning Yahgans, was a missionary who had volunteered to work among the Fuegans (a mission that ended in failure) and a young naturalist, Charles Darwin, whose name was to become inseparably linked with the famous round-the-world voyage of the *Beagle*. Not only did the expedition prove FitzRoy's ability as an outstanding seaman and hydrographer, but it was from observations made during the journey that Darwin amassed evidence for his epoch-making theory of the evolution of life. Few voyages have had such momentous and far-reaching results.

A few years after the *Beagle's* voyage the French navigator Dumont D'Urville reconnoitered the Strait of Magellan and urged his own government to take over the territory through which it ran. Interest grew in this remote but strategically important part of the world. In 1840 two paddle steamers, *Chile* and *Peru*, of the Pacific Steam Navigation Company, rounded Cape Virgins and there began a regular steamship service between Europe and the west coast of South America. Stimulated by this activity, General Manuel Bulnes, president of the Republic of Chile (which had gained her independence from Spain in 1817), sent a mission to take possession of the strait and to form a settlement at Port Famine. And so it came about that on September 21, 1843, the *Ancud*, a 30-ton schooner under the command of Juan Williams, came to anchor near the site of Sarmiento's old city. In the afternoon of that day, in a ceremony strangely reminiscent of Ladrillero's small expedition nearly three centuries before, the Chilean flag was raised above the shores of Magellan's Strait. The event forestalled by one day the arrival of a warship, the *Phaeton*, sent by the French government for the same purpose.

Restored buildings at Fort Bulnes where Captain Juan Williams raised the flag of Chile on the Strait of Magellan in 1843. In the background, over the Strait, are the spectacular snow-capped peaks of Mount Sarmiento in the Darwin Range of Tierra del Fuego.

Port Famine was renamed Fuerte (Fort) Bulnes in honor of the president. A few years later, however, owing to a lack of good water, the little settlement was shifted some fifty miles along the coast to the north, to the site of present-day Punta Arenas. By that time the government of Argentina had formally established her claim over eastern Patagonia.

4

The Eastern Steppes

One of the lowest passes through the southern Andes is the Paso de Pérez Rosales. It crosses from Peulla, on the eastern shore of Lake Todos los Santos, to the great Nahuel Huapí National Park of Argentina. The route is becoming increasingly popular, for it has a well-deserved reputation for its wonderful lake and mountain scenery. I remember the journey well, for it is one that first led me into the great plains of Patagonia and showed me the immense contrasts between one side of the Andes and the other.

Late one February afternoon I came to Peulla, having traveled that day by road and by boat from the Pacific coast near Puerto Montt. The weather had been perfect. The volcano of Osorno, a classic snow-capped cone, rose in a cloudless sky above the intensely blue waters of the lake. Across the sun-splashed stillness blossoms of *ulmo* trees gave a dusting of white to the forest fringes. From the little wooden jetty at Peulla a short walk took me to a handful of chalets and the single hotel set amidst the trees.

The valley at Peulla is hemmed in by mountains and steep forest. The approach is either across the lake or along a narrow unsurfaced road that winds down through the trees from the head of the pass. There are fields along the floor of the valley with thickets of bamboo and a profusion of ferns growing in moist places. Wild barberries were in flower at the time of my visit, and their beads of glistening yellow blossoms made a pleasing sight among scarlet fuchsias.

The sun shone brilliantly during those first days of my journey. There was a sense of that warm peacefulness of mountains in late summer. One morning I crossed the Tronadore River above Peulla, riding on the ox cart of some wood-

White blossoms of ulmo, *the eucryphia tree*

cutters bringing logs to the village for the winter. The riverbed was wide, but now at the end of the dry season the pearl-colored waters raced and glistened through channels among broad stretches of gray shingle and sand. On the far side I followed a path through grassy glades where yellow butterflies, similar to our northern sulfurs, were very abundant. Further on, by a still backwater, there opened up views of tree-clad ridges backed by towering snow-capped peaks. Graceful beeches came down to the edges of grassy places left by the falling waters, and among these were lapwings and little groups of buff-necked ibis. These and other birds— snipe, austral blackbird, rayadito (similar to the chickadee), and the caracaras or carrionhawks—were to accompany me now through to the southern tip of the continent.

The weather changed all too soon. The next morning was cool with low clouds and I accordingly made my way over the frontier into Argentina. I barely saw Mount Tronadore, whose 11,000-foot peak towers over the pass; only once did the mists roll back to reveal sunlit ice and black rock far above the forest. Over the border it remained gray with the mountains hidden on all sides. In a chilling wind I boarded a launch for the short distance across Lake Frias to a point where a track led over a narrow neck of land to the shore of Lake Nahuel Huapí. From there a trim steamer took me along fiordlike arms of water, across the lake, to San Carlos de Bariloche, one of the best-known towns of northern Patagonia.

The scenery around Bariloche, the center of the national park, matches the splendor of the famous Lake District of southern Chile. It is a country of mountain, lake, and forest; of flowers and of Alpine chalets with varnished timbers and shingled roofs. German settlers brought their own style of

59

architecture, and their traditional wooden-faced buildings fit pleasingly into these Andean landscapes.

From Bariloche I took the road which winds south, keeping close among the lakes and mountains to El Bolsón. The mountains at first were jagged and broken. Trailing plants, called mutisias, with brilliant lilac and orange star-shaped flowers, clambered over the scrub and low beeches. Gradually, the hills became more rounded and the vegetation sparser and drier-looking. From Epuyen on to Esquel I was among rolling plateaus, with small trees only in the shelter of

Church at Llao-Llao on Lake Nahuel Huapí in northern Patagonia

Foothills of the Andes at Esquel

valleys; and so the scene changed to the open country of eastern Patagonia.

Cradled among the hills of Esquel are many lakes and moist depressions where ducks and overwintering geese gather. Sheldgeese are among the most characteristic birds of the Patagonian plains. One species, the snow-white kelp goose, belongs to the coasts, but three others are pre-eminently birds of the land. These are the upland or Magellan goose, the ruddy-headed goose, and the ashy-headed goose. All are rather similar, with short narrow bills and barred under-

61

plumage, and best told apart by the coloring of the head (the upperparts of the male upland goose are white). At the end of the southern summer, these birds fly north from their breeding grounds on the coast and islands of Tierra del Fuego and Magellan's Strait and congregate—often in flocks of many hundreds—wherever there is suitable grazing. They run into trouble with farmers, for in such numbers they compete with livestock for food. I was told that during the early years of sheep farming, the killing of foxes (which feed on the eggs and young of the geese) and the clearance of land in suitable areas for pasture resulted in an extraordinary increase in the numbers of these birds. Travelers of the time spoke of flocks darkening the skies. Now, however, the wild geese are by no means as widespread as they were, and it is not too soon for thought to be given to their protection.

Perhaps the most peculiar bird of the Patagonian plains is the rhea—the South American version of the ostrich. This is Darwin's rhea, the smaller of two species (the other keeps more to the tropical lowlands, from the pampas of Argentina to central Brazil). They are wary birds, moving away with an ever watchful eye as one approaches. Even the skilled Tehuelche hunters (in the days before they had horses) were said to use a camouflage of feathers over their head and body when stalking rheas. One morning I watched a small flock in a valley near Esquel. They made an unforgettable sight, with their ruffled gray plumage, standing among the maroon pads of giant thistles and grasses turning to their autumnal colors. Sadly, for they are said to be protected, these birds are still hunted, although for no better reason that I could discover than that their feathers make fine dusters. The eggs, cooked in their shells in the ashes of a fire, are considered a great delicacy by the mounted herdsmen of Patagonia.

The grasses had cast a mantle of silver and gold over the hills of Esquel. It was still March, but hot and dry enough for the wind to lift the soft crumbling soil into dishevelled vortices, which careered over the dusty outskirts of the town. Rains had left their mark, cutting long channels that looked as if a giant hand had run its nails through the land. In the shelter of these places grew many flowers, of kinds I was not to see elsewhere: a host of low annuals, the hoary-leaved mullein, and evening primroses—whose scent I was to come across time and again on the still air of these ravines. The

The mara or Patagonian cavy, a harelike rodent, inhabits the dry eastern plains of Patagonia.

level areas of the plateau were gently undulating, with rounded mats of low vegetation, coarse grass and thistles, and here and there little mounds broke the monotony of the country. Among these raised places, especially where it was sandy, there were colonies of tucotucos, one of the most characteristic mammals of the Patagonian plains.

Secretive dwellers—similar in habits and appearances to the pocket gophers of North America—tucotucos emerge from their burrows at night to feed on roots and grasses. Normally one is only aware of their presence by their holes honeycombing the ground and faint musical notes coming from the burrows. These calls have been likened to the sound of beating on tiny anvils, a curious medley of chinks and trills that are made when someone walks about overhead—or when anything else equally untoward goes on outside the tucotucos' world. These small rodents have grayish fur, short tails, diminutive ears, long digging claws and, for some reason, bright orange front teeth. Once they were so abundant that it was quite awkward to walk or ride over land where their holes riddled the ground. Now, in sheep-grazing areas, they have been largely trampled out of existence. There are several species, one living far south among the cool glades of the forests of Tierra del Fuego.

My way from Esquel led eastward into the flatter and more open tablelands of central Patagonia. There was a monotony to the dry featureless plains which stretched to the horizon beneath dull skies. The withered plants and ragged clouds had a certain stylized beauty of their own, but I found there nothing really warm or welcoming. It was a melancholy land and my thoughts turned to the nomadic tribesmen whose home it had been not so many years before.

The Tehuelches did not go without a bitter struggle. Any

Clock tower and statue of Julio Argentino Roca in San Carlos de Bariloche. General Roca was responsible for the final subjugation of the fierce Indian tribes of the pampas and southern Argentina and later became President of his country.

Argentinian schoolchild knows of Roca's "Conquest of the Desert." This was General Julio Argentino Roca who during the years 1879–83, at the head of 5,000 men, finally subjugated the turbulent Indians of the Patagonian plains and laid the way open for settlers from Europe.

The settlement of eastern Patagonia was far from easy. Violent winds, irregular rainfall, and cold winters all made life difficult, especially to people who had come from the relative warmth of countries bordering the Mediterranean. Spaniards, Yugoslavs, Arabs, Germans, Poles, Rumanians, and Britons all arrived among the early immigrants and settled along the floodplains of the great rivers—the Chubut, Chico, Deseado, and Santa Cruz—that cross the territory from the west to the east. Along these valleys, often separated by hundreds of miles from each other, the settlers cultivated ribbon-like oases, sowing crops and tending livestock. At the same time Chilean sheep farmers moved northward from the region of Punta Arenas and settled along a fertile depression at the foot of the Andes. Such a pattern of settlement tended to impose considerable isolation upon the different groups, which resulted in a remarkable array of communities that even today reflects the diverse origins of its inhabitants. Among the first and in many ways most individualistic of these were the Welsh.

In 1865, 152 emigrants from Wales came to settle in the valley of the Chubut River. With little experience to guide them, they suffered great hardships until it was realized that

Opposite: *Willow, tamarisk, and poplar trees fringe a water canal in Chubut. Only by irrigation has the cultivation of crops become possible in this arid region of eastern Patagonia.*

only by irrigation could a living of any kind be wrested from this land. The impact of drought and flooding—archenemies of settlers in desert regions—was reduced by an elaborate system of irrigation canals. Cereals were sown, sheep and cattle raised and, after many setbacks, trading links established with other colonists to the north. Of great interest, looking back on these achievements, was the creation of an idealistic community, a "little Wales beyond Wales," with its own language, schools, chapels, and newspaper. Welsh is still spoken there. But, after over a century, it is now dying out, and of about 20,000 people of Welsh descent living in the Chubut Valley less than half speak their mother tongue. Yet, features of their cultural heritage, such as the *eisteddfods* or traditional festivals of Welsh music and literature, have been retained as part of life in this Patagonian valley.

In 1868, the Argentinian government gave a concession to Captain Luis Piedrabuena for the colonization of land along the Santa Cruz River. To help further establish a claim over her still little-known Patagonian territory, military titles were given to Tehuelche Indian chiefs who had aligned themselves with the authorities in Buenos Aires. One enterprising chief, however, named Casimiro, taking advantage of rival claims between the two governments, sought, and obtained, a military rank from Chile as well. Border disputes, generally, had tended to linger on with the Chileans. Problems had arisen on several occasions, and it was only with the treaty of October 22, 1881, that Argentina finally recognized Chile's claim to the Strait of Magellan. At the same time the mutual frontier was agreed on, which followed the water shed of the Andes and divided Tierra del Fuego between the two nations.

Argentinian Patagonia today is divided into the provinces of Neuquén, Río Negro, Chubut, Santa Cruz, and the Terri-

Above: *The town of Gaiman, founded by Welsh settlers, in the Chubut Valley. Beyond the valley rises the bleak tableland of the Patagonian steppes.*

Below: *The Welsh school, built in 1906, at Gaiman.*

tory of Tierra del Fuego. Throughout this vast area, larger than the states of Arizona and New Mexico combined, there are less than a million people. The main towns on the coast are Comodoro Rivadavia, Viedma, Puerto Madryn, Río Gallegos and, in Tierra del Fuego, Ushuaia and Rió Grande. Inland, along the foothills of the Andes, several resort centers have grown up in recent years, the best-known being San Martín de los Andes, Bariloche, Esquel, and Calafate. In these towns and along the main river valleys live the great majority of the people of Patagonia today, descendants of many nationalities linked by the Spanish language and by ever-increasing ties with the federal capital of Buenos Aires.

Between the water courses that cross to the Atlantic lies the series of gigantic plateaus that constitute the wild scrubland best known as Patagonia. Unlike the pampas, which it joins to the north, the Patagonian steppe rises in a succession of wide terraces reaching a height of four or five thousand feet near the mountains. Much of the surface is covered with tracts of shingle, 200 feet deep in places, which lay under the sea many tens of millions of years ago. The pebbles are cemented together by a kind of aluminous soil, and so peculiar are these remains of ancient seabeds that they are known by geologists simply as The Patagonian Formation. Toward the west, the shingle is replaced by granite and reddish-colored porphyry (an igneous rock, such as granite, in which large detached crystals are embedded); and in many parts, particularly near the Chico and Santa Cruz rivers, there are also vast sheets of volcanic basalt and lava. Often in the hollows of the plains are broad shallow lakes, heavily impregnated with soda and other mineral salts, which are the feeding places of flamingos. Apart from these lakes and the valleys, where the soil is richer, the general aspect of the plains is one of arid desolation. The vegetation is made up of wiry grasses and

70

such typically wind and drought resistant plants as the low, fleshy-leaved *jume, quilimbai* (a bush with yellow flowers and important as a food plant for sheep), and a berberis (calafate) whose sweet fruits were known to early explorers as Magellan's grapes. The few townships of the steppe come to life at sheep-shearing time and during the short holiday season, and then subside into somnolence for the rest of the year, lulled by the creaking of waterpumps and the varied sounds made by the wind.

The Atlantic coast, which I reached at Río Gallegos, brought me back among prolific wildlife. Here, the rise and fall of the tides, which are among the greatest in the world, leave vast stretches of intertidal mud and seaweed exposed which are a haven for marine and wading birds. Abundant mussel beds support huge flocks of oyster catchers, conspicuous black-and-white birds whose shrill calls are heard at most hours of the day, mingling with the gaggle of sheldgeese. The white kelp ganders with their dark mates are a common feature, resting on the shelving shingle at high tide. Offshore, seaweed or kelp beds float in gently rolling masses, where sea ducks gather in great numbers. Several kinds of cormorants, notably the king, rock, blue-eyed, and the widespread bigua or neotropic, also thrive along these food-rich waters. Cape pigeons, southern fulmars and other petrels move up from the antarctic winter and, together with penguins and elephant seals, bring a polar touch to the seas of southern Patagonia.

The little Magellanic penguin occurs all along the coast. During the winter, from April to September, it is at sea feeding on squid and small fish, insulated from the cold by a tight coat of feathers and a protective layer of blubber. Nesting begins in the spring when the penguins gather in huge colonies, or rookeries, at suitable places where they can

71

clamber ashore. At one colony I visited, at Punta Tombo on the coast of Chubut, an estimated half a million pairs of birds come together each year for nesting. The eggs are laid under bushes or in shallow burrows dug by the males.

Several early voyagers spoke of the huge penguin rookeries and of the importance of these birds in provisioning their ships. At a colony near the estuary of the Deseado River Thomas Cavendish "powdred three tunnes of Penguins for the victualing of his shippe." One wonders if they made good eating with their notoriously fishy habits. But people in those days were evidently not so particular. "A man hath an excellent stomach here," wrote the worthy Sir John Narborough, ". . . I can eat Foxes and Kites as savourily as if it were Mutton."

Penguins, so graceful and adroit in the sea, appear thoroughly out of their element on land, shuffling along like old men in oversized carpet slippers. On one occasion I watched a procession of these birds moving toward the sea. Rolling slightly and looking most carefully at the next few steps to be made, they wandered along in a bemused way as if they were a little the worse for drink. Once in a while one toppled over and tried going along for a spell on all fours. As with other penguins, they often appear highly amusing with their droll antics.

The eastern coast of Patagonia contrasts strikingly with the western, there being scarcely an island of any size throughout its length of 2,000 miles. Instead, a gently sweeping coastline, ringed by cliffs, forms the characteristic succession of gulfs that border the Atlantic. The low Valdés Peninsula, connected by a narrow stretch of land with the coast of Chubut, is exceptional—a unique geographical feature of this coast.

The cliffs offer many protected coves, where sea lions

The flippers of penguins are stiff, flattened versions of wings which the birds use to drive themselves through the water.

gather to haul themselves out of the water. Elephant seals come ashore too, particularly on the remote beaches of the Valdés Peninsula. The bulls, to the tip of their outstretched flippers, reach a length of twenty or more feet, making them the largest of all the seal family. These huge beasts were once found in great numbers around the coasts of California, as well as on many islands in the southern oceans and Antarctic Sea. Seal hunters slaughtered countless thousands for their oil, and it is good to know that the Argentinian government has made strict laws for the protection of this colony in Patagonia.

A cold current flowing northward from the Falkland Islands is responsible for the sea mists that often cling to the coasts and offshore waters of eastern Patagonia. Inland parts are comparatively rainless, but the dry atmosphere there

73

Sea lions on the Valdés Peninsula

allows sudden extremes in temperature. At any time of the year it can fall below freezing, and in winter winds and driving snow can make life very uncomfortable to anyone venturing up into the exposed plateaus. Fortunately, the severe spells are usually short in duration and, except in a few bays, the sea never freezes. Winds are seldom absent, blowing in from the west and southwest, whispering among the wiry stems, and rising at times to a buffeting blast.

The few days I spent at Río Gallegos before going on to Tierra del Fuego were clear and windy. I was reminded of blustery weather in the fall on our northern Atlantic coasts. Somewhere in the distance rose gentle hills, their slopes clothed in soft hues of buff. Nearer at hand, wind-flecked waters, fast-moving clouds, and the deserted waterfront below the town all spoke of the harshness of this land of extremes.

74

5

Fiords and Glaciers

From north to south the Andes span more than one-sixth of the circumference of the Earth. From their slopes one can survey the Caribbean, the steaming forests of the Amazon, and the sub-Antarctic islands of southern Patagonia. As spectacular as are the northern tropical parts of the range, to my mind they rarely match the wild splendor of the south.

For an understanding of the geography of this region one has to imagine a partly submerged chain of mountains. The different ridges are separated by deep valleys which were carved originally by great bodies of ice, the glaciers, as they moved along them. Following a gradual tilting and lowering of the land, the sea flowed into these valleys to form fiords. Where these arms of the sea joined each other channels and islands appeared. Now imagine all this stretching over a thousand miles and one can have some idea of the immense scale and complexity of the south Chilean coast.

One of the surprising features of the southern Andes is the presence of two great ice caps—the only examples of their kind outside the polar regions. These are unbroken mantles of ice and snow which fill the high valleys and form a barrier for

A still day on the Baker Channel in Aisén Province

nearly 600 miles along the backbone of Patagonia. The sides of these ice fields are festooned with glaciers. These glaciers end at the heads of the valleys and fiords in the west, while those in the east display their fronts in an uninterrupted series of lakes of all shapes and sizes. Some of these lakes, such as Argentino, Viedma, and O'Higgins, with long narrow arms running between steep forest-clad mountains to the glaciers, are places of extraordinary beauty.

76

At Lago Argentino, the source of the Santa Cruz River, the government of Argentina has set up the spectacular Glaciers National Park. There, from the town of Calafate on the southern shore of the lake, visitors can travel to the Moreno Glacier where a 100-foot wall of ice stretches two miles across the water. The glacier itself is some ten miles long, curving down from the mountains as a great tongue of ice, riven and scarred with crevasses. At its front the ice is broken and convoluted into fantastic shapes. Once in a while massive pieces of ice break away with a sound like thunder and float away majestically as icebergs.

Ice-cliffs of the Moreno Glacier on Lake Argentino

The blue color of glaciers is due to the compression of ice under its own tremendous weight. The more compacted ice becomes, the more its crystals absorb the red and yellow wavelengths of light. The blue rays are then free to be reflected on their own, giving wonderful shades of color in the translucence of ice.

Most of the glaciers in the Andes—and throughout the world—are shrinking, a process known by glaciologists as recession. The Moreno Glacier is a striking example of the opposite process—a glacier where the rate of accumulation of snow and ice in its upper parts exceeds the loss due to melting at its front. In 1949 a wall of ice was found to be advancing into beech forest, moving imperceptibly but destroying trees with irresistable force. Several times the glacier front has pushed right across a part of the lake creating a dam behind which the waters have risen inundating large areas of forest. Dangers arise when this barrier breaks and the sudden release of ice-impounded waters causes flooding of farming and grazing land lower down the valley. This happened following a dramatic build-up of waters in 1941–42.

At no other comparable latitude in the world is there such a profusion of glaciers. Several factors are responsible for this. It has to be sufficiently cold and there must be enough precipitation—but these conditions exist elsewhere without glaciers forming in the same way. The main reason is that it is cool practically all the time in southern Chile and there is little evaporation. Even in summer there is not much warmth to melt the accumulations of snow and ice. The permanent snow line on Mount Burney, for instance, is under 3,000 feet; and there are few days without some rain, sleet, or snow. Rainfall on parts of the western coast of Patagonia has been recorded as high as 18 feet a year.

The 8,000-foot Paine Mountains of southern Chile owe their shapes to the scouring action of glaciers in the Ice Age.

However inhospitable the climate, the southern Andes have become an ever-growing attraction to mountaineers. To those keen on climbing in remote areas, scattered peaks rising like islands amid the mist and wind of the ice caps offer an irresistible challenge. The ascents of Mount FitzRoy, the Paine Mountains, and Cerro Torre have provided dramatic chapters in the history of mountaineering. Cerro Torre, a 10,000-foot pinnacle of ice-encrusted rock, has become the epitome of the unattainable peak. Climbed twice, in 1959 and 1971, with the aid of mechanically drilled holds, the ascents have become a source of controversy among climbers, many of whom disagree with the use of such aids. The southern, and larger, ice cap was crossed for the first time in 1956; and several remarkable journeys have been made there in recent years using man-hauled sledges. The interior of the Darwin Range, on an uninhabited peninsula in Tierra del Fuego, was completely unknown until the 1960s. Other smaller and more remote island ranges have remained virtually inaccessible to man behind their barrier of tempestuous seas.

As mountains go, the Andes are fairly young, having been formed in the last 100 million years from a folding and faulting of the Earth's crust. They betray their still youthful and unsettled state in continuing volcanic activity and earthquakes. Mounts Burney, Hudson, Huequi, Minchinmávida, and Corcovada (the latter three in Chiloé) are all volcanoes that have showed signs of activity in the past 150 years. The whereabouts of others have been intriguing mysteries. Mount Lautaro, on the Southern Ice Cap, was located in 1933 after reports of ash eruptions had circulated ever since the discovery of the great lakes toward the end of the last century. An expedition in 1973 found that volcanic activity in the region was more widespread than at first believed. Among sea chan-

80

The only reported eruption of Mount Burney was in 1910. Today there is no obvious sign of volcanic activity and the higher peaks are covered with a mantle of ice.

nels to the north of the Gulf of Peñas travelers today may see sheets of fine yellowish pumice floating on the water. They have been there since the 1950s, carried backward and forward with the tides; and no one, I was told, has yet traced their origin.

Chilean Patagonia comprises the provinces of Magallanes (which includes the southern and western parts of Tierra del Fuego), Aisén, and Chiloé. Roads from the Chilean capital of Santiago run only as far south as Puerto Montt, the main

A Chilote islander

town of the province of Llanquihue, and across to the Island of Chiloé. Beyond, there are no land connections, and the only way to drive to Punta Arenas on Magellan's Strait is through Argentina.

The Island of Chiloé, generally considered as the northern outpost of Patagonia, is separated from the mainland on the north by the narrow Strait of Chacao. It has long been inhabited by man. Its people today, descendants of the indigenous Indians and European settlers, are a hardy and independent race. The island is 110 miles long and has an area a little less than that of Puerto Rico. The inland parts are mountainous with very dense forests in the south and west. The country to the east has been largely cleared to make farmland, where wheat and potatoes are grown, and the scenery there with its villages is reminiscent of New England. The principal towns are Ancud and Castro. The last Spanish garrisons were expelled to the island in 1818 when the rest of Chile seceded to independence. For a further eight years the Island of Chiloé remained loyal to Spain, but it finally fell and became incorporated into a province of the new republic.

Although woodcutters and farmers have been extending their activities southward from the Island of Chiloé, they have had little impact so far on the South Chilean Islands as a whole. Indeed, a great part of this region has been left empty since the decline of the canoe-Indians. Between Chiloé and Puerto Natales in the south the only real settlements are at Puerto Aisén and on the Yelcho and Baker rivers, where gaps through the mountains provide access to moderately sheltered and drier valleys inland, and at Puerto Edén on Wellington Island.

Wellington Island, 400 miles to the south of Chiloé, is a

barren, 100-mile tract of mountain, glacier, swamp, and forest, deeply cut by fiords. Behind a group of low wooded islands on the east is the cluster of buildings that forms Puerto Edén, important not only as the home of the last surviving group of Alacalufs but as the sites of meteorological and air-route stations of the Chilean government. Apart from this little enclave, which dates back to 1936, there is not much to distinguish the coast of Wellington from the rest of the 800 miles of mist-enshrouded mountains that border the sea route between Punta Arenas and Puerto Montt. Small groups of fishermen and occasional seal and otter hunters travel through this region, but their activities are seasonal and on the decline.

Mussel fishermen in southern Chile

The temperate rain forests which line these coasts are of particular interest to naturalists. The trees are of few species and dominated, in the lower parts, by two evergreen beeches, the guindo and (in the north of Patagonia) the coigue. At higher elevations, the guindo is replaced by deciduous species, the lenga and the ñire or antarctic beech. The conifers are represented by a kind of cypress and, in the north, by a larch locally known as the alerce. Forests of huge alerces spread over to the eastern slopes of the Andes, where trees in places are reputed to be 3,000 years old. Not far from Esquel is the Alerces National Park, which was established to ensure the preservation of some of these forest giants. The Winter's-bark, related to the magnolia, with pretty but rather small white flowers, is another common tree of the forests of the western part of Magellan's Strait and the Channels. It derives its name from Captain Winter, who accompanied Sir Francis Drake on his voyage around the world and who tried the use of its bark as a condiment to help relieve scurvy among his crew.

The vegetation under the trees is usually very dense. In northern Patagonia, kinds of bamboo (called chusquea) form dense thickets which make parts of the forest virtually impenetrable. Even in the more open spots, the undergrowth is thick and damp, with rotting branches and carpets of mosses and lichens. Several prickly shrubs, among them barberries and the holly-leaved *Desfontainea*, make traveling even more difficult. Yet, dismal as these forests are, there are some really beautiful flowers. This is the home of the fuchsia, which has been grown for many years as an ornamental plant in our gardens. Few flowers that I have seen can match the coicopihue (a near relative of the copihue, the national flower of Chile) in its natural setting. In the darkness of these forests,

with the wind roaring through the tops of the trees overhead, its delicate bell-shaped flowers of rose magenta have an almost ethereal quality. The waxy crimson and yellow blossoms of *Desfontainea*, too, are very striking, and a favorite haunt of the southernmost hummingbird in the world.

The range of the green-backed firecrown extends southward into Tierra del Fuego. In the north, this little hummingbird is equally at home in the hot valleys of the Atacama Desert. Surely, no other bird of a comparable size tolerates such extremes of climate! A member of the parrot family, the austral parakeet, is also found in these cold Patagonian forests. It attracted the attention of several early voyagers, among them van Noort in 1599 who referred to the "fair woods in the Strait of Magellan full of parrots." The largest woodpecker in South America—black, crimson-crested, and closely related to the ivory-bill that once inhabited the forests of the southeastern United States—also lives in these woodlands of southern Chile.

Opposite: *Dense thickets of bamboo bordering a beech forest in northern Patagonia*

Right: *The austral parakeet, a bird of the southern beech forests*

In 1973 I spent several weeks on Mount Burney. During journeys through the forest, my frequent companions were dark birds, the size of a house wren, with short erect tails and outsized feet. These were Andean tapaculos. In fact, I rarely saw the birds, for, like the several species of tapaculo in Patagonia, they were experts at keeping out of sight. Instead, I was aware of their presence by their calls, merry and surprisingly loud sounds that seemed to emanate from the very ground around me. Only by waiting silently for some time could I catch sight of one, moving about like a diminutive black clockwork chicken among the draperies of moss.

Inland on Mount Burney there stretched several miles of forest and peat bogs. As the ground rose, so the trees became progressively smaller. At their upper limits, the deciduous beeches formed low spreading thickets, no more than a few inches high. Winds swept and scoured this country, shaping the trees, raising spindrifts of snow on the glaciers, and keeping much of the animal life down in the shelter of the valleys.

Two birds, however, I shall always associate with the wildest and most exposed parts of the Patagonian mountains. The seedsnipes are short-billed partridgelike birds peculiar to the moorlands of the southern Andes. It is wonderful to hear their sonorous calls in the dusk of a still evening as a covey skims low over the open ridges of the mountains. The high country, too, is the home of the condor. The name of these huge graceful flyers of the vulture family is indelibly linked with the Andes. Now, alas, they are becoming all too rare, having been exterminated from many of their former haunts.

The huemul is a medium-sized deer of the mountains of Patagonia. It lives as far south as the Muñoz Gamero Peninsula, moving down to the protection of the forested valleys in wintertide. In areas uninhabited by man it is still delightfully tame and trusting. The smallest deer in the world, the chest-nut-colored pudu, not much bigger than a hare, also lives among the temperate forested slopes of Patagonia. Among the other mammals are two species of fox, several opossums, the puma, and many rodents. In the forests of Chiloé lives the rincolesta, a small undistinguished-looking marsupial (mammals which carry their young in a pouch), but of great interest to zoologists as it is closely related to a group of animals that have long been extinct.

The coasts and waterways of Patagonia are the home of sea otters, fur seals, and nutrias, all of which are hunted for their fur. Marine birds, despite their relative abundance, are little disturbed by man. The kelp beds provide rich feeding

Black-necked swans are equally at home on sea channels as on the freshwater lakes of Patagonia.

grounds for cormorants, gulls, and a host of ducks. The loggerhead or steamer ducks are among the most curious inhabitants of this region. They are large heavy birds which splash over the water using their wings like paddles—a clumsy but effective means of locomotion. One species has lost completely its ability to fly. Loggerheads feed on mollusks, shrimps, and crabs. Another spectacular member of the duck family is the black-necked swan, which breeds among the lakes and estuaries of the far south of the continent. About April these graceful birds fly northward to spend the winter months on the pampas and among the sheltered waterways of central and northern Patagonia.

6

Land of Fire

The three Yahgan Indians returned by Robert FitzRoy to Tierra del Fuego provoked a wave of interest in this hitherto little known part of the world. In December, 1832, when *H.M.S. Beagle* sailed once more to the southern coast of Isla Grande there were no European settlers anywhere in the archipelago. The only inhabitants were nomadic tribesmen who had advanced little beyond a Stone Age existence. As we have seen, their fires alone had given seafarers the impression of a populous land and a name for the country of its inhabitants—Tierra del Fuego, Land of Fire.

It must have been a curious scene as Fuegia Basket and her two companions went ashore at the quiet bay of Wulaia on Navarino Island to begin life again among their untutored relatives. Dressed in fine clothes and laden with an assortment of household goods (which included tea trays, chamber pots, and white linen), the protégés of FitzRoy evidently did not make a very good impression. Indeed, Jemmy Button, who appeared to have forgotten much of his native tongue, had great difficulty even in making himself understood. With them went the young and rather taciturn Richard Matthews who had been sent by the Church Missionary Society to continue the instruction of the Fuegans and, if possible, to find a way of spreading further the elements of Christian teaching. Five days later, safely installed on land, Matthews and his charges were left to their own devices.

A little over a week later FitzRoy returned to see how they were faring. He was dismayed to find that the Fuegans had overrun the camp, taking anything that they fancied and giving Matthews a terrible time with their incessant demands for gifts, pulling his beard, and pelting him with stones. In vain had his three pupils tried to restrain them. The missionary promptly and thankfully returned on board, and it must have been a sad moment for FitzRoy when he realized how much his efforts had been wasted in trying to bring a new way of

Northern limits of the antarctic beech forest in eastern Tierra del Fuego

life to these people. However, he departed not altogether without hope, and promised to return. A year later, when the *Beagle* was again in those waters, it was found that even Jemmy, who in London had taken such pride in his dress and smart appearance, had finished with civilization. For clothes he wore a piece of blanket round his middle, his face was painted, and his hair had grown long and matted. He greeted FitzRoy courteously, however, and took luncheon on board in his old style, but nothing would induce him to change his ways again.

A few years later the Patagonian Missionary Society was formed in London. At its head was a former naval captain, Allen Gardiner, who had decided to devote the latter part of his life to preaching the Gospel among uncivilized tribes. After visiting many parts of the world, he finally chose Tierra del Fuego as the scene for his work. Gardiner's subsequent efforts, on behalf of the Fuegans, make a story of incredible suffering and hardship. At the end of their resources, the victims of the recurring hostility of the Yahgans, Gardiner and six companions died in the winter of 1851 on a lonely beach in the southeast of Isla Grande.

George Pakenham Despard took over the work of the Patagonian Missionary Society. A base was established at Keppel Island in the Falklands to where some of the Yahgans were taken in order that their language might be learned. Despite this, further tragedies followed. In 1859 the crew of the mission schooner was murdered at Wulaia by the uncompromising Yahgans. In this attack it was suggested that the now ageing Jemmy Button was in some way involved, but this was never proved. The ship was plundered and only one of the crew, the cook, survived to tell the tale.

The activities of the society (renamed in 1864 the South

American Missionary Society) continued at the Keppel settlement under the leadership of Waite Stirling, who later became first Bishop of the Falkland Islands. There, Thomas Bridges, the adopted son of the Reverend Despard, worked on his dictionary of the Yahgan language. Steady progress was made from that time and in 1869 a mission was finally established on Tierra del Fuego. The site chosen was at Ushuaia, on the Beagle Channel, where there was a sheltered harbor and a level expanse of open ground suitable for stock-raising and limited cultivation.

Life at the new settlement did not remain peaceful for very long. Fortunes, however, now began to weigh against the Yahgans and their neighbors inland, the Onas. Sheep ranchers arrived and began to annex the land of the Indians. The discovery in 1876 of gold along Magellan's Strait brought fresh immigrants, some less scrupulous than others, and in 1884, following the delineation of the southern limits between Argentina and Chile, the Argentinian government set up a subprefecture alongside the mission at Ushuaia. About that time diseases, alien to the Indians, began to sweep through and to decimate their ranks. So susceptible were the Onas and so quickly were they dying that many of the survivors were rounded up at one stage and shipped across to a newly-established mission of the Salesian Fathers on Dawson Island. There, herded together under unnatural conditions, the ravages of disease only increased . . . and so, in one way and another, the stage was set for the final tragedy that followed. It is to the Reverend Thomas Bridges and to his son, Lucas Bridges, that we are indebted for an account of the events that led to the decline of the Fuegan Indians.

The great majority of the early settlers—gold-washers,

Ushuaia lies at the foot of the mountains on the northern shore of the Beagle Channel.

sealers, skin traders, who came to exploit the resources and inhabitants of the archipelago—flit briefly and anonymously through the pages of Fuegan history. One figure, however, emerged above the rest, and his rise to become the virtual dictator of Tierra del Fuego fits into the aura of fantasy that surrounds early pioneer settlements.

Julius Popper was the son of a Rumanian merchant. He studied as a mining engineer at Paris, saw service at some stage in the army, and was an accomplished linguist. He also had remarkable organizational ability. Accompanied by a band of well-armed men he traveled south from Buenos Aires in the vanguard of the gold rush in the 1880s. Crossing Magellan's Strait, he reached San Sebastián Bay on the Atlantic and there discovered rich bands of a black gold-bearing sand. He devised a way of working the deposits mechanically and very quickly made a success of his prospecting. Increasing his claims, Popper employed more and more armed guards and eventually assembled what was in effect a private army. Miners at that time were more or less obliged to protect their own concessions, for there was hardly any law-enforcing agency along the hundreds of miles of beaches being worked by prospectors, but the more powerful Popper became the more tyrannical he grew. He drew up his own mining laws, deported or shot intruders, and issued his own stamps and currency—the latter cast in pure gold, bearing on one side a crossed pick and shovel and on the reverse the simple legend "Popper." As he had his own shipping as well and owned most of the farms in Tierra del Fuego, there was very little anyone, including the government-appointed governor at Ushuaia, could do to oppose him. Even in Buenos Aires he enjoyed great prestige, and when this remarkable man died in 1897 he was widely acclaimed by the Argentinian nation. Among the many projects which he had planned were those for a line of steam tugs for the Strait of Magellan, a system of telecommunications and improved maritime services for the south of Argentina, and an expedition to explore the neighboring territories of Antarctica.

The principal and largest island of Tierra del Fuego is Isla Grande. About the size of Denmark, it has the same topographical diversity as Patagonia to the north of the Strait of Magellan: the western and southern parts bordering the mountains are humid and forested, while the rest of the island is relatively flat and dry. Before the end of the nineteenth century, the estancias of sheep farmers had spread across the northern non-forested part of the island, and set the pattern for the future economic development of the archipelago as a whole.

96

Other large islands in Tierra del Fuego are Navarino, Hoste, Clarence, Desolation, and Santa Inés. Only the Chilean island of Navarino and the eastern tip of Hoste, together with Dawson and three small islands at the entrance to the Beagle Channel, are inhabited. The outer and more exposed parts in the south and west are not inhabited and it is not conceivable at this time that they ever will be.

A good motor road runs across Isla Grande. In the north it passes through open grasslands, where the visitor sees flocks of sheldgeese and sheep grazing together in the fields; from Río Grande, the center of a growing oil industry, the road runs along the coast and then turns south into the forests and mountains that divide the island. Where the forest begins,

Preparing smelt at a canning factory at Porvenir in Chilean Tierra del Fuego

Upland or Magellan geese grazing at the edge of antarctic beech forest. The heads and necks of the ganders are white, contrasting with the darker color of the females.

tongues of deciduous antarctic beech spread into rolling grassland and follow higher ground above the lakes and rivers. It is an extraordinarily beautiful country, especially in early April when the trees are burnished with red and gold autumnal tints. Further south the road skirts Lake Fagnano and then winds through the mountains to drop down on the far side to Ushuaia.

Few towns in the world have a more dramatic setting than Ushuaia. Ringed by impressive snow-capped mountains, immersed in the recent history of its settlement, and a base for Antarctic research programs, it is scarcely surprising that it is the goal for an increasing number of visitors traveling to the southern tip of the continent. Along the Beagle Channel rise the little known peaks of the Darwin Cordillera—Mount Darwin, over 8,000 feet high, and Mount Bové with its hanging glaciers and mantles of forest clinging to its lower slopes.

There is something oddly chaotic about these Fuegan forests, with their ragged appearance, lichen-draped trees, and the ground littered with a tangle of dead and graying branches. For some reason fallen branches do not rot as quickly as elsewhere and the interior of these places brings to mind the uncanny regions of a Gothic tale. Many times I have wandered in the stillness of these strange woodlands, trying to picture the troops of guanaco coming to find shelter, and their hunters, the Onas, before white man came to this land.

The guanaco are still there, high up beneath the glaciers on Mount Bové and haunting the forest fringes of the island. To see these graceful animals in their natural setting is an unforgettable experience, and it is to be hoped that they will always remain a part of the Fuegan scene.

One memorable day, in the forests of Tierra del Fuego, I had my first opportunity to watch guanaco. It had been warm and still, with barely a breath of wind to stir the pale tresses of lichen on the trees. Caracaras, the long-legged hawks of the region, had followed me from time to time, and I had heard their croaking calls and the hollow whistling beat of their wings. But there had been little to disturb the soli-

Ushuaia, capital of the Argentinian Territory of Tierra del Fuego, attracts many visitors during the summer months of December to March.

tude. Suddenly, ahead of me, in a glade of the forest, there were eight or nine guanacos. Elegant versions of the llama, the first thing to impress me was the freshness and the uniformity of their coloring—cinnamon brown and snow white, with gray faces and chocolate brown tails. For long moments they gazed attentively round and round at the woods, heads high, ears and eyes alert for the least sign that might give away my whereabouts. Every now and then one took a few deliberate steps forward, intimidatingly, and then turned round as if to see what the others thought of its temerity. At length, after one or two false starts, they made off through the forest in an easy loose-limbed canter, weaving among the fallen branches.

Liquid eyes, long eyelashes, and a woolly fleece conceal the most querulous of dispositions. Male guanacos are belligerent and frequently fight among themselves. Intrusion by one troop into the territory of another is sufficient reason for a breach of the peace, an incident quickly flaring into an articulate scuffle of kicks, bites, and squeals. The South American camel tribe as a whole (which includes the vicuña as well as the guanaco and its domesticated forms, the llama and alpaca) also have the ability to spit the contents of their stomachs, which they do both accurately and with apparent relish into the face of an adversary, treating man in the same disdainful way if they feel the need arises. But in the wild, where man is concerned, they are usually wary animals, uttering a shrill quavering neigh and withdrawing at the first sign of danger to a distance where they can survey in safety the cause of disturbance. At times, however, their curiosity, or a peculiar brand of truculence, takes the upper hand, and on these occasions the animals throw caution to the winds, indulging in such absurd antics as prancing and squealing, as if they were deliberately drawing attention to

100

themselves. I had a soft spot for guanacos, with their odd ways, and later on, during a journey across the uninhabited mountains of southern Tierra del Fuego, I was frequently glad of the diversion of their company.

The guanaco was formerly abundant throughout Isla Grande. Following a decline at the turn of the century, its numbers are now increasing, but on Navarino its status is very uncertain owing to the presence of a growing human population and the shortage of meat generally on the island. In an attempt to alleviate this latter problem, a dozen reindeer were brought as a breeding stock by the Chilean authorities at the end of 1971 (from South Georgia, where they had been successfully introduced some years before), and while this new experiment could be of interest and some utility it is not likely to augur well for the future of the guanaco on the island.

Although the biologist draws no broad distinction between the wildlife of the two sides of Magellan's Strait, it is interesting that several well-known animals have not extended, or no longer extend, into Tierra del Fuego. These include the puma or mountain lion, the huemul, vizcachas (bushy-tailed rodents related to the chinchillas), and the armadillos. Among the birds is the rhea. On the other hand, two fur-bearing animals, the muskrat and beaver, have been brought by man and are now an established part of the Fuegan fauna. Introduced in the late 1940s, the beaver spread rapidly among the swampy beech-clad valleys of the south of Isla Grande.

Being so far south (the same latitude as Labrador in the north) the Fuegan year is divided into marked seasons. This is more noticeable on the sheltered side of the mountains, in the north and the east, where the majority of people live. The winters there are generally calm and windless. Snow

Black-crowned night-heron: a bird of the coasts of Tierra del Fuego

falls and settles in large flakes, and there are many weeks of enduring coldness. In early September, as soon as the ice is off the ground, the wild geese return, to be followed by little flocks of ibis—buff-headed, gray-winged, whose strident voices always bring for me most vivid memories of this southern land. By mid-October, the spring is well advanced. New grass appears, the lambing season begins, and green leaves spread through the forests of antarctic beech. A few crops are sown, such as oats and clover for fodder, and vegetables in gardens protected from the wind. Long summer days follow when flowers brighten the fields and the calafate, wild currants, and crowberries come into fruit. By the middle of March there is already an autumnal touch to the air. Summer birds such as swallows and lapwings gather to move north, and along the coasts arrive the winter immigrants from the far antarctic south.

7

Emerging Patagonia

Following the treaty of 1881 the southern borders of Argentina and Chile were defined dividing Patagonia between the two countries. Although the line was understandably vague in places, and subsequent disputes over the ownership of several areas had to be settled by arbitration, the basic frontier remained. This left the Strait of Magellan and humid mountainous areas in the west and extreme south to Chile, while the greater part of the relatively flat and arid steppes remained in Argentinian hands. In Tierra del Fuego the frontier ran across the middle of Isla Grande and then followed the Beagle Channel eastward to the Atlantic.

A year or two after the settlement was formed at Ushuaia sheep were taken to Isla Grande. They did well in the cool Fuegan climate and sheep farming soon became the basic livelihood of settlers. Estancias spread northward beyond the mountains, absorbing grazing lands of the guanacos and the old hunting grounds of the Onas. In 1893 the Sociedad Explotadora de Tierra del Fuego was formed. This company had its own freezing works and, leasing over three and

103

a half million acres of land on Tierra del Fuego and the mainland, became the largest sheep-farming organization in the world. By the turn of the century several companies were regularly exporting consignments of wool and frozen meat from Punta Arenas.

The number of sheep throughout Patagonia, including Tierra del Fuego, grew to around twenty million, and although this number has fallen in recent years sheep farming remains at the basis of the economy of the region. The traditional estancia is usually an isolated farmstead, lying in the shelter of a valley or fold in the hills, and comprising a collection of low corrugated buildings surrounded by corrals and a windbreak of planted trees. The sheep runs extend over the open steppes and on the larger ranches cover many tens of thousands of acres.

The principal breed of sheep in Tierra del Fuego, and throughout southern Patagonia generally, is the New Zealand Corriedale. This is a hardy dual-purpose breed, providing meat and good quality wool. In the north of Patagonia, especially along the Negro River, merinos, better known for their fine wool, are raised. The flocks are brought down to the valleys for the winter and during hard periods are driven into the protection of corrals. The chief danger is from snow drifting and burying the animals in the dips and hollows where they shelter, but even when this occurs they can survive surprisingly long periods huddled together (two weeks or more), providing the snow remains light and not too compacted for the animals to breathe. Normally, they are able to forage enough food for themselves and the provision of winter-feed becomes necessary only under exceptionally severe conditions.

The sheep are tended by mounted shepherds, known as

Above: *An estancia in the upper Santa Cruz Valley*

Below: *The mainstay of the economy of Tierra del Fuego and eastern Patagonia*

gauchos. These are the legendary herdsmen of the pampas and the plains of Patagonia, depicted in stories with their spirited horses, silver-studded saddles, spurs, and richly-embroidered clothes. The life of the gaucho is in reality a lonely one. In Patagonia this means long days under the open sky, tending widely scattered flocks and looking after miles of boundary fencing. The clothes normally worn are simple, the most typical garment being wide pleated trousers called *bombachos*, which are held by a colored waistband, and have the legs tucked into high boots of soft leather. The saddle, too, used for day to day work is far from ornate. It consists of two lengths of padded leather with stirrups attached which hang on either flank of his horse. Two or three sheepskins thrown on top—over the strips of hide that hold the stirrup supports together—complete a warm and comfortable saddle. On long journeys the gaucho carries with him a small horn or vessel for brewing maté tea, the popular drink of southern South America.

Even in winter the shepherds are seldom idle. The sheep have to be guarded from foxes (the red fox, the larger of two native species), and on the wilder estancias pumas come down once in a while to raid flocks. Lambing begins in October, and from then on the men are kept very busy. Shearing is in full swing in January and February and is the time of greatest activity on the estancias. On the larger farms as many as 3,000 sheep are clipped a day for their wool. During the southern fall sheep and lambs are rounded up to be taken to the freezing factories and slaughtered for meat. Traditionally, the animals are driven in flocks, perhaps three or four thousand at a time, herded by men on horseback and a team of dogs. The journey from outlying estancias may take a week or two, with nights by the roadside for the men, dogs, and horses, and the sheep guarded in pens provided at regular intervals by farms along the way. With improving road communications the tendency is for sheep to be transported more and more by trucks; in addition many tens of thousands of living sheep are now exported every year in special ships to Europe and the Middle East.

Modern technology has given new impetus to mining operations, for both oil and minerals. This is more on the Argentinian side where a network of roads exists and several railways run in from the coast. Coal is mined at Río Turbio

Meat freezing factory near Puerto Natales on Last Hope Inlet

in Santa Cruz province and carried by rail to the port of Río Gallegos. Many of the workers at the mine, which is near the frontier, come from the town of Puerto Natales in Chile. For many years the Chileans successfully worked their own coal deposits (although not of the best quality) on the island of Riesco. This venture became uneconomical with the gradual disappearance of coal-burning ships and the development of the Río Turbio mines with their easier access to the coast on the east. Other mining operations, although of small size, continue among the South Chilean Islands, notably for lime, marble (in the archipelagos of Diego de Almagro and Madre de Dios), and for copper, lead, manganese, and antimony ores. Deposits of kaolin (for ceramics) and iron ore are worked in Chubut.

One summer's day in 1907 two engineers were drilling for water in Comodoro Rivadavia, then a small cluster of houses beneath dry eroded hills on the coast of Chubut. Instead of water, so badly needed in this parched country, oil was found and there began the industry that was to bring Comodoro to the forefront of Patagonian towns. Today some 6,000 wells are in operation in the eastern part of the provinces of Chubut and Santa Cruz and make this the most important oil-producing region of Argentina. Large reserves of natural gas are also being tapped in the south of Santa Cruz and in Tierra del Fuego and piped northward to Buenos Aires. The entire production of petroleum and natural gas in Chile at this time comes from deposits alongside the Strait of Magellan; exploitation on a commercial scale began in Tierra del Fuego in the 1940s.

A substantial part of the timber used in Chile comes from Patagonian sawmills. In the north, forest products are

Oil rigs at Comodoro Rivadavia

transported to Puerto Montt and then by sea, road, and rail to
the central provinces of the country. Further south trans-
portation is the great problem and the trade is, to some
extent, subsidized by the Chilean government which pro-

Left: *A thriving industry has grown around the exploitation of beech forests in the south of Isla Grande.*

Right: *Much of the timber from sawmills on Lake Fagnano is transported by road to Ushuaia, then by sea to Buenos Aires.*

vides transport by naval vessels to the markets in Punta
Arenas. In Argentina, forests around Lake Fagnano and
along the southern coast of Isla Grande in Tierra del Fuego
are being exploited commercially. The timber trees in
greatest demand are the beeches, lenga and guindo, the
cypress and, in the north of Patagonia, the alerce and
manihu.

Settlers exploiting forest resources in southern Chile
have been able to move to a new area and simply begin
felling trees. A mechanical saw and a pair of oxen with
which to haul the logs to the mill are all that is really necessary for a family to set up in the lumbering business; and
there are a good many of these small family concerns scattered along the coasts south of Chiloé and along the western
arm of the Strait of Magellan. The great problem with this
form of uncontrolled exploitation is that large areas are left
stripped of their covering of trees, bringing the danger of
soil erosion and considerable disturbance to native wildlife.
In addition, the burning of forests has continued year after
year, largely to try to convert land into pasture. Fortunately,
controls and reforestation schemes are now being brought
into force by governmental authorities.

Cropping the rich sea resources has growing importance
in Patagonia. Catches include oysters (in the province of
Chiloé), mussels, sea urchins, and a kind of large spider
crab known as the centolla. The centollas are netted in
fairly deep water from late October to January and taken
to canning factories at Porvenir, Punta Arenas, and on Dawson Island. The flesh of these crabs, which resembles
lobsters', makes them a great delicacy and represents one of
the chief exports of the Chilean province of Magallanes.
Smelt, sprat, mullet, and haddock are among the fishes that

111

are netted commercially by small fleets operating from ports in southern Argentina and along the Strait of Magellan. The production of animal sea foods in Magallanes in recent years has been about 10,000 tons annually.

The only agricultural and horticultural pursuits that have become possible in Patagonia on a large commercial scale are centered along the valleys of the Negro (on the northern borders of Patagonia) and Chubut rivers. There, fruit and vegetable growing has become successful, notably with the exportation of frozen apples and pears. Irrigation in the Chubut valley has created a fertile strip some three to ten miles wide alongside the river. Neat farms and fields bordered with poplars, willows, and tamarisk trees make a striking contrast to the line of bare hills on either side. Potatoes, beans, and processed alfalfa (a cattle food) have been exported to Chile and the Falkland Islands. In addition, wheat, barley, sweet corn, grapes, pumpkins, and a variety of root and salad crops are grown for home use.

The opening of the Florentino Ameghino Dam in 1963 resulted in improved irrigation methods in the lower Chubut valley (although an attendant problem arising from an increasing salification of the soil has yet to be solved) and heralded a new era of industrial development in eastern Patagonia. Hydroelectric energy now serves the expanding oil fields and petrochemical works of Comodoro Rivadavia and a variety of entirely new industries in the region. Among these are textile and plastic factories at the rapidly growing commercial center of Trelew. A more specialized industry is the manufacture of agar-agar—again utilizing available energy and manpower of the lower Chubut valley. Used in biochemical research and the preparation of antibiotics, agar-agar is made from seaweed, the raw material being

112

Hydroelectric plant below the Florentino Ameghino Dam

brought by road from Bustamente Bay to the factory at Gaiman. It is the largest processing plant of its kind in South America. A huge aluminum producing factory is being developed at Puerto Madryn, where a new deep-water pier has been built by the Argentinian government.

For very many years Punta Arenas played a key role in the economic development of Patagonia. The port grew up as the main trading center for the south, becoming more closely tied to markets in southern Argentina than with the rest of Chile. The state of communications at the time was sufficient reason for this. Motorized transport had hardly been devel-

113

oped, and in addition there was a lack of good ports along the tide-harassed coast of southern Argentina. The growth of Comodoro Rivadavia and, more recently, Puerto Madryn—both with good harbors—and the construction of roads linking the eastern Patagonian towns with the capital, Buenos Aires, inevitably brought a shift in trade routes.

Punta Arenas suffered a depression which reached its nadir in the early 1950s. Chilean meat freezing plants had to stop production as the supply of sheep from ranches on the Argentinian side of Patagonia drew to a close. The manufac-

Comodoro Rivadavia, center of the rich oil-producing region of eastern Chubut and Santa Cruz

ture of tallow (formerly an important industry in Magallanes) ceased when the last factory was closed in 1950. Small steamship companies, many having been in operation for over half a century, went out of business, together with the associated shipyards and coal mines. Many people left the province to seek employment in the central parts of the country and over the border into Argentina.

The last two decades, however, have seen some regrowth in the importance of Punta Arenas. The expansion of the petroleum industry, and the reorganization and growth of farming activities have been in part responsible for this; but the town has yet to regain its former grandeur and international standing.

Tourism is the new aspect of the economy which is bringing the greatest changes to Patagonia. Five airlines serve the region as a whole, and at all the main centers of population, hostelries, restaurants, and other facilities are being provided for visitors. The journey to Ushuaia, at the southern tip of the continent, has become a holiday drive for motorists from as far north as Uruguay and Brazil. In Argentina the federal government exercises jurisdiction over the many national parks of Patagonia, which include beautiful areas of the Andes in the provinces of Neuquén, Río Negro, Chubut, and Santa Cruz and the National Territory of Tierra del Fuego. Elsewhere there is skiing, and fishing and hunting for such introduced species as salmon, trout, hare, wild boar, and European red deer. Reserves exist to protect seals, penguins, and strange petrified forests in the provinces of Chubut and Santa Cruz. In Chile a series of national parks stretches from Aisén province and the celebrated Paine Mountains to the Lake of the Swans (near Porvenir) in Tierra del Fuego.

Winter at Lake Argentino in the Glaciers National Park

Year by year an increasing number of visitors come to see the many and varied scenic beauties of Patagonia. Even with civilization spreading rapidly across the habitable parts, one easily forgets there the march of time—whether it is beneath the wide skies in the east or among the lonely waterways of the Pacific, where the Andes reach into the sea.

Scientific Names of Plants and Animals Mentioned in the Text

Alerce: *Fitzroya patagonica*
Armadillo: *Zaedyus pichiy* and *Chaetophractus villosus*
Bamboo: *Chusquea culeu, C. quila* and *C. tenuiflora*
Barberry: *Berberis buxifolia, B. darwinii* and *B. ilicifolia*
Blackbird, austral: *Curaeus curaeus*
Butterfly, sulfur: *Colias vauthieri*
Calafate: *Berberis buxifolia*
Caracara, crested: *Polyborus plancus*
Celery: *Apium australe*
Centolla: *Lithodes antarcticus*
Coicopihue: *Philesia buxifolia*
Coigue: *Nothofagus dombeyi*
Condor: *Vultur gryphus*
Copihue: *Lapageria rosea*
Cormorant: *Phalacrocorax albiventer, P. magellanicus, P. atriceps* and *P. olivaceus*
Cress (food-plant collected by canoe-Indians): *Cardamine glacialis*
Crowberry: *Empetrum nigrum*
Currant: *Ribes magellanicum*
Cypress: *Austrocedrus chilensis*
Desfontainea: *Desfontainea spinosa*
Fern (used as roofing material by canoe-Indians): *Blechnum magellanicum*

119

Flamingo: *Phoenicopterus chilensis*
Fox: *Dusicyon culpaeus* (Patagonian red) and *D. griseus*
Fuchsia: *Fuchsia magellanica*
Fulmar, southern: *Fulmarus glacialoides*
Goose: *Chloephaga poliocephala, C. rubidiceps, C. picta* and
  C. hybrida
Guanaco: *Lama guanicoe*
Guindo: *Nothofagus betuloides*
Gull, kelp: *Larus dominicanus*
Heron, black-crowned night-: *Nycticorax nycticorax*
Huemul: *Hippocamelus bisulcus*
Hummingbird, green-backed firecrown: *Sephanoides*
  sephaniodes
Ibis, buff-necked: *Theristicus caudatus*
Jume: species of *Suaeda*
Kelp: *Macrocystis pyrifera*
Lapwing: *Vanellus chilensis*
Lenga: *Nothofagus pumilio*
Loggerhead or steamer duck: *Tachyeres pteneres*
  (flightless) and *T. patachonicus*
Manihu: *Podocarpus nubigenus*
Mara or Patagonian cavy: *Dolichotis patagona*
Maté: *Ilex paraguensis*
Morel: *Cyttaria darwinii*
Mullein: species of *Verbascum*
Mussels: *Mytilus chilensis* and *M. magellanicus*
Mutisia: *Mutisia retusa* (lilac-flowered) and *M. decurrens*
  (orange-flowered)
Ñire or antarctic beech: *Nothofagus antarctica*
Nutria: *Myocastor coypu*
Otter, sea: *Lutra felina*

120

Oyster catcher: *Haematopus leucopodus* and *H. ater*
Parakeet, austral: *Enicognathus ferrugineus*
Penguin, Magellanic: *Spheniscus magellanicus*
Pigeon, Cape: *Daption capense*
Poplar: *Populus nigra*, introduced to Patagonia
Primrose, evening: species of *Oenothera*
Pudu: *Pudu pudu*
Puffball (Tierra del Fuego): *Lycoperdon giganteum*
Puma: *Felis concolor*
Rayadito: *Aphrastura spinicauda*
Rhea: *Pterocnemis pennata*
Rincolesta or Chilean rat opossum: *Rhyncholestes raphanurus*
Quilimbai: *Chuquiraga avellanedae*
Seal, elephant: *Mirounga leonina*
Seal, fur: *Arctocephalus australis*
Sea lion: *Otaria byronia*
Seedsnipe (on Mount Burney): *Attagis malouinus*
Skunk: *Conepatus humboldtii*
Smelt: *Odostethes platensis*
Snipe: *Gallinago gallinago*
Swallow: *Tachycineta leucopyga, Notiochelidon cyanoleuca* and *Hirundo rustica*
Swan, black-necked: *Cygnus melancoryphus*
Tapaculo, Andean: *Scytalopus magellanicus*
Tepú: *Tepualis stipularis*
Tucotuco: *Ctenomys magellanicus*
Ulmo: *Eucryphia cordifolia*
Vizcacha: *Lagidium viscaccia*
Willow (Chubut Valley): *Salix humboldtiana*
Winter's-bark: *Drimys winteri*
Woodpecker: *Campephilus magellanicus*

Index

123

126

ROGER PERRY

was born and has his home at Enfield, in England. During his school years, his interest in animals and wild places took him to some of the more remote parts of Europe—to the Alps, the Pyrenees, and the mountains of Norway. After serving in the army, he entered Christ's College at Cambridge University, and graduated in zoology. He first traveled in South America during 1957-58, when he joined a group from his university climbing and studying plants in the Colombian Andes.

After four years in England with the Natural History Unit of the British Broadcasting Corporation, Mr. Perry left on a journey to the forests of the Upper Amazon. In 1964, he was assigned to the Galápagos Islands in Ecuador as a UNESCO specialist in wildlife conservation. After six years in the Galápagos he made three extended journeys to Patagonia, and these travels form the basis of this present book.